Conducting the Network Administrator Job Interview

IT Manager's Guide for Network Administrator Job Interviews with Network Administrator Interview Questions

Adam Haeder

10-04

This book is dedicated to Tina, Erin and Ethan, for making it all worthwhile.

--- Adam Haeder

Conducting the Network Administrator Job Interview

IT Manager's Guide for Network Administrator Job Interviews with Network Administrator Interview Questions

By: Adam Haeder

Copyright © 2004 by Rampant TechPress. All rights reserved.

Printed in the United States of America.

Published by Rampant TechPress, Kittrell, North Carolina, USA

IT Job Interview Series: Book # 4

Series Editor: Don Burleson

Editors: Janet Burleson, John Lavender, and Linda Webb

Production Editor: Teri Wade

Illustrations: Mike Reed

Cover Design: Bryan Hoff

Printing History: February 2004 for First Edition

Network Administrator, Network Administrator7, Network Administrator8, Network Administrator8i, and Network Administrator9i are trademarks of Network Administrator Corporation. *Network Administrator In-Focus* is a registered Trademark of Rampant TechPress. Flame Warriors illustrations are copyright © by Mike Reed Illustrations Inc.

Many of the designations used by computer vendors to distinguish their products are claimed as Trademarks. All names known to Rampant TechPress to be trademark names appear in this text as initial caps.

The information provided by the authors of this work is believed to be accurate and reliable, but because of the possibility of human error by our authors and staff, Rampant TechPress cannot guarantee the accuracy or completeness of any information included in this work and is not responsible for any errors, omissions, or inaccurate results obtained from the use of information or scripts in this work.

ISBN: 0-9744355-7-0

Library of Congress Control Number: 2004101890

Table of Contents

Using the Online Code Depot

Your purchase of this book provides you with complete access to the online code depot that contains the sample tests and answers.

All of the job questions in this book are located at the following URL:

rampant.cc/job_net.htm

All of the sample tests in this book will be available for download in a zip format, ready to load and use on your database.

If you need technical assistance in downloading or accessing the scripts, please contact Rampant TechPress at info@rampant.cc.

Conventions Used in this Book

It is critical for any technical publication to follow rigorous standards and employ consistent punctuation conventions to make the text easy to read.

However, this is not an easy task. Within Network Administrator there are many types of notation that can confuse a reader. It is important to remember that many commands are case sensitive, and are always left in their original executable form, and never altered with italics or capitalization.

Hence, all Rampant TechPress books follow these conventions:

Parameters – All application parameters will be in *lowercase italics.*

Commands – All commands and program output will be in **lowercase bold.**

Programs & Products – All products and programs that are known to the author are capitalized according to the vendor specifications (IBM, DBXray, etc). All names known by Rampant TechPress to be trademark names appear in this text as initial caps. References to UNIX are always made in uppercase.

Acknowledgements

This type of highly technical reference book requires the dedicated efforts of many people. Even though I am the author, my work ends when I deliver the content. After each chapter is delivered, several Network Administrators carefully review and correct the technical content. After the technical review, experienced copy editors polish the grammar and syntax. The finished work is then reviewed as page proofs and turned over to the production manager, who arranges the creation of the online code depot and manages the cover art, printing distribution, and warehousing.

In short, the author played a small role in the development of this book, and I need to thank and acknowledge everyone who helped bring this book to fruition:

John Lavender, for the production management, including the coordination of the cover art, page proofing, printing, and distribution.

Teri Wade, for her help in the production of the page proofs.

Bryan Hoff, for his exceptional cover design and graphics.

Janet Burleson, for her assistance with the web site, and for creating the code depot and the online shopping cart for this book.

Linda Webb, for her expert page-proofing services.

With my sincerest thanks,

Adam Haeder

Preface

After interviewing hundreds of candidates for network administrator-related positions, we are aware that it is getting harder to locate and retain qualified network administrator professionals. You must cull the best fit for the job from hundreds of résumés. Success depends upon knowing exactly which skills you need, and verifying that each candidate possesses acceptable levels of those skills.

That's where this book can help you. For both the new IT manager and the seasoned VP, the levels within the network administrator professional position will be explained to illustrate screening and interview techniques. Some common misconceptions will be clarified about the network administrator professional position and tips will be provided on how to interview a candidate for a network administrator professional position.

Large numbers of networking neophytes are obtaining certification through various vendor certification programs. This glut of certified professionals makes it more important than ever to evaluate every network administrator professional job candidate's experience and working knowledge.

Few IT managers, especially in smaller companies, have extensive formal training in interviewing and hiring techniques. Most interviewers' primary full-time responsibility will lie elsewhere. It is a fact that most IT managers do not even have a clear idea of the skills and personal characteristics their candidate should possess, much less an effective process for screening potential employees. Yet, nothing is more crucial to the success of the organization than doing everything possible to insure that the selected candidate is the best fit for the available position.

This book will provide effective techniques for finding committed employees who are able to function at a high level on the job. By eliminating guesswork, and rejecting the random hit-or-miss approach that is based on the instincts of the interviewer and little else, the employer can hire promising candidates with the confidence that the odds are stacked in his favor.

To help find, hire, and retain suitable networking professionals, background evaluation tips will be provided for identifying the best candidates. For the technical interview, sample technical questions and answers are also provided. A non-technical evaluation section is provided to help determine whether the candidate's personality is a good match for the organization, able to integrate seamlessly with your shop's particular culture.

Of course, there is no magic formula for determining if a candidate can perform properly, and no single screening test to ensure that you will properly evaluate a candidate's ability. However, if the employer and candidate are properly prepared, then filling the position successfully becomes much less chancy.

It is our hope that this book will provide you with an indispensable tool for identifying, interviewing, and hiring top-notch network administrator professionals.

The intention of this book is not to provide a comprehensive technical exam, and the technical questions in the code depot are only intended to be examples. The only way to accurately evaluate the technical skills of a job applicant is to employ the services of an experienced person and conduct an in-depth technical interview and skills assessment.

Also note that the expected answers from the questions are highly dependent upon the version of the product and the candidates' interpretation of the question. We have tried to make

---

the questions as version neutral as possible, but each new release of every product brings hundreds of changes and new features, and these example questions may not be appropriate for your version. An experienced technical person should always administer the interview questions presented in this book.

Evaluating the Network Administrator

Introduction

As networks continue to grow and increase in complexity, hundreds of thousands of companies, from mom-and-pop grocery stores to multi-billion dollar corporations, have seen the need for professional network administrators. This mushrooming need has created a vastly disparate job pool. Job skills range from network administrator with PhDs in Information Systems from top U.S. universities and 20 years' experience, to semi-literate network administrator trainees with 90 days' experience.

The result of the explosive growth of the networking industry is a two-tiered job market. Many top-rated universities teach network administration as part of their undergraduate CS or IT curriculum and produce professionals for career tracks in large corporations. At the same time, trade schools and community colleges produce hundreds of thousands of IT graduates. No matter what the economic climate, large corporations actively recruit their entry-level talent for their mission-critical networking roles from prestigious universities.

Preparing the Network Administrator Job Offering

One of the points that we repeatedly make is that top-notch network administrator professionals are hard to find and well-compensated, while mediocre network administrator professionals are easy to find and hire.

On the high end, professionals with over 10 years' experience and graduate degrees typically command salaries ranging from $75,000 to $150,000 per year, depending on geographical location. For consultants with a broad exposure in mission-critical areas, the sky is the limit. For example, a successful consulting company can charge $200/hour for experienced on-site networking consultants.

On the other end of the spectrum, we see overseas networking trainees who will work remotely from Bangalore, India for as little as $10/per hour, and CCNA certified beginners who are desperate for a chance to learn networking on your multi-million dollar production environment.

The first step in hiring a networking professional is determining the level of skill you require and preparing an incentive package. If your network is mission-critical, then a seasoned network administrator professional is your safest choice, and people with high skill levels often require incentives to abandon their employers.

Preparing the Incentive Package

If you want a top-notch senior network administrator, you may be surprised to find them in short supply, even in a down job market. While every manager knows that salary alone cannot guarantee employee loyalty, there are a host of techniques used by IT management to attract and retain the top-notch network administrator.

Network professionals like the latest hardware and software!

In addition to a competitive salary, some of the techniques used to entice potential Network Administrators include:

Flex time – Burnout can be a real problem among the Network Administration professionals who must typically work evenings and holidays to maintain the computer systems. Many companies offer formal comp-time policies or institute a four-day workweek, allowing the Network Administrator to work four, 10-hour days per week.

Telecommuting - Many Network Administration professionals are allowed to work at home and only visit the office once per week for important face-to-face meetings.

Golden handcuffs - Because a high base salary does not always reduce attrition, many Network Administrator managers use yearly bonuses to retain employees. Golden handcuffs may take the form of a Management by Objective (MBO) structure, whereby the Network Administrator receives a substantial annual bonus for meeting management expectations. Some companies implement golden handcuffs by paying the employee a huge signing bonus (often up to $50,000) and requiring the employee to return the bonus if he or she leaves the company in less than three years. However, don't be surprised to find that some competing companies will reimburse the Network Administrator to repay a retention bonus.

Office perks - Since many senior Network Administration professionals command salaries commensurate with those received by corporate vice presidents, some senior Network Administrators are offered private offices and company cars.

Fancy job titles - Because Network Administrators command high salaries, many are given honorary job titles. These include "fellows" titles such as the Apple fellow, whereby the corporation grants special privileges to Network Administrators who have been granted fellow status. Other professional titles include vice president of operations, chief technologist, and the new job title (used by Bill Gates), chief software architect.

Specialized training – Networking professionals are commonly rewarded by attending conferences and training classes. An entire industry has grown up around these large events. The Geek Cruise Line is typical of this movement, offering technical conferences on hot topics in network administration,

Java, and Perl, combined with an ocean cruise. Companies pack these cruise ships with their networking professionals, sailing to exotic destinations in Alaska, Hawaii, and the Mediterranean.

Defining the Required Job Skills

A number of networking professionals mistakenly believe that the network administrator's job is purely technical. In reality, the Network Administrator must be an "ace" of all IT functions, because he or she has ultimate responsibility for overall network design, implementation, maintenance, performance, and security. Excellent interpersonal skills and communicative abilities are required, as well as technical skills, for the network administrator's close involvement in all phases of project development.

Remember, knowledge of networking is not enough. An understanding of operating systems and computer-science theory is imperative as well. That is why employers like to hire network administrators who also have a background in computer science, information systems, or business administration.

It's critical to remember that networking certification tells employers only that the job candidate successfully passed a certification test on the technical aspects of networking. In the real world, certification is just one of many criteria used to evaluate a network administrator job candidate. Other criteria include the following:

Excellent Communication Skills - The network administrator is the central technical guru for the shop. He or she must be able to explain networking concepts to all developers and programmers using the network. In many shops, the network administrator is also a manager and is required to have excellent communication skills for participating in strategic planning and architectural reviews.

Formal Education – Many employers require network administration professionals to have a bachelor's degree in computer science or information systems. For more advanced positions, many employers prefer a master's degree in computer science or a Master's in Business Administration (MBA).

Real-World Experience - This requirement is the catch-22 for newbies who possess only a CCNA certification. A common complaint of people who have the CCNA certification but no job experience is that they cannot get experience without the certification, and they cannot get a job without experience. This is especially true in a tight job market.

Knowledge of Network Administrator Theory - In addition to mastering the technical details, the successful network administrator must have an understanding of network design.

Basic IT Skills

Because the network administrator is often called-upon to perform critical projects in the IT department, a broad background is often desirable. Much of this basic IT knowledge is taught in academic Computer Science and Information Technology programs. Non-Network Administrator job skills include:

System Analysis & Design – Many network administrators must take an active role in the analysis and design of new systems. Hence, knowledge of system analysis, CASE tools, Entity-relation modeling and design techniques enhance the network administrator's scope of ability.

Physical Disk Storage – Understanding of disk hardware architecture, cache controllers, and disk load balancing are beneficial to any network administrator.

Data Security Principles – An understanding of data security issues, including role-based security, is highly recommended, especially for US Government positions.

Change Control Management – In many cases the networking professional is charged with the task of implementing change control and insuring that changes to the production network are properly coordinated. Knowledge of third-party change control tools, such as the UNIX Source Code Control System (SCCS), is beneficial.

Now that we understand the basic skills, let's talk about certification. The Cisco Certified Networking Associate and Certified Networking Professional exams identify candidates who have mastered specific technical areas within network administration. However, as interviewers frequently discover, possession of the certification is no guarantee that a candidate has real network administration expertise.

📖 **Code Depot Username = reader, Password = raffles**

Cisco Certified Professionals

Lured by the promise of big bucks, thousands of ordinary blue-collar people have managed to complete "Network Administrator boot camps" that teach them how to pass the Cisco exams. From shoe salesmen to auto mechanics, people are getting certified by Cisco without the appropriate IT background.

The Value of Cisco Certification

Starting with the obvious question, what is the value of Cisco certification? Considering that Cisco exams cost $125 each and that some certifications require up to five exams, and factoring in the cost of books, classes, and other study materials, Cisco certification can be a sizable investment. However, the potential rewards can make that investment worthwhile.

Here's the catch – Cisco certification alone is not a guarantee that anyone will find employment in network administration. The Cisco certification is just one of the credentials valued by prospective employers.

The Cisco certifications are the most popular of all networking certifications. Originally, the only Cisco certification available was the Cisco Certified Internetworking Expert (CCIE), a much sought after certification with an extremely high failure rate. However, Cisco has expanded the program due to the explosive demand for networking professionals. Cisco Certified Networking Associates (CCNA) and Cisco Certified Networking Professionals (CCNP) are the two popular lower-level certifications available.

Network Administrator Characteristics

While many IT shops have hundreds of technology workers, retention efforts are normally focused on technical gurus, whose knowledge of the company's systems is not easily transferred to replacements.

In many shops, network administrators typically serve many roles. In addition to traditional duties, the administrator is often called upon to serve as a system architect, an Informaticist (a functional IT professional who possesses an MS in computer science and is also trained in professional areas, such as medicine or accounting), a database administrator, or a system administrator.

The following attributes are signs of a top-notch network administrator professional:

Has earned at least one professional degree or certification - Possessing a degree such as MD, JD, MBA, MSEE, or CPA, in addition to a computer science or IT degree, makes an employee a valuable asset, one difficult to replace in the open job market.

Has graduated from a competitive university – Networking professionals must be self-starting and highly motivated to be effective, and this is often indicated by entrance to competitive universities with rigorous admission standards. These schools include most Ivy League schools, especially MIT, and universities with stellar reputations in Information Systems such as Purdue, the University of Texas, the University of California at Los Angeles, the University of San Diego, and the University of California at Berkeley.

Active in the networking community - Many good networking professionals participate in local user groups, present techniques, and publish in many of the networking-related periodicals.

Is recognized as a Network Administrator expert - A sure sign of a Network Administrator all-star is someone who gets in front of audiences by publishing a book, writing a magazine article, or appearing as a conference speaker.

Possesses irreplaceable knowledge of an institution's enterprise systems - If the employee serves in a mission-critical Network Administrator role, such as chief architect or senior networking analyst, a vacuum in the IT department may be created by that employee's departure.

A good Network Administrator will demonstrate persistence!

Sample Job Sheet for a Network Administrator

Applicants for any networking job are expected to meet all the requirements in mission-critical areas, including education, experience, certification, writing credits, personal characteristics, and legal standing. Here is an example Network Administrator job requirement sheet from an actual corporation:

Sample Network Administrator Job Sheet

These are the minimum job requirements for the position of Senior Network Administrator. The HR department will pre-screen all candidates for the following job skills and experience.

Education

Persons with Masters Degrees, Doctoral degrees, and Ivy League graduates are desired. At a minimum, the candidate is expected to possess a four-year degree from a fully-accredited university in a discipline such as Computer Science, Software Engineering, BA or MBA in Information Systems (from an AACSB accredited university), or Engineering (electrical, mechanical, or chemical).

Work Experience

The Network Administrator candidate is required to have a minimum of five years of full-time, progressive experience in LAN and WAN administration and management.

Network Administrator Certification

The Network Administrator candidate must have earned a networking certification at some time in the last five years.

Publishing and Research

The candidate should show demonstrable interest in publishing networking research as evidenced by participating in user groups and publication of articles, books and columns. These include:

- Books. Networking technical books or any other recognized academic publication company.

- Articles for academic journals. For example, the Journal of the IEEE and the Journal of Information Systems.

- Conference papers. Writing papers and presenting at conferences such as Networld+Interop.

- Articles in trade publications. Writing an article for a trade publication such as SysAdmin, LAN Times or Network Computing.

Personal Integrity

This position requires securing mission-critical applications and accessing confidential data, and all candidates are required to sign a waiver to disclose personal information.

The Network Administrator candidate must have no history of acts of moral turpitude, drug use, dishonesty, lying, cheating, or theft.

USA Citizenship

We are unable to sponsor H1-B foreign consultants. Therefore, candidates must provide proof of US citizenship or appropriate visa.

Additional Specialized Skills

The following specialized skills are desired:

- Masters or Doctorate degree from a major university
- An active US Secret, Top secret or Q-level security clearance
- UNIX System Administration HP/UX, Solaris or Linux.

As we can see, Network Administrator positions have requirements that vary widely, and it is up to the IT manager to choose those qualities that best suit the position.

Conclusion

This chapter has been concerned with identifying the job requirements and preparing an incentive list. Next, let's take a look at how to evaluate the Network Administration professional for specific job skills.

Qualities of a
Desirable Candidate

The evaluation of the résumé is a critical part of the selection process. In a tight job market, it is not uncommon to receive hundreds of résumés, and it is the job of the HR or IT manager to fairly and efficiently pre-screen applicants and only forward qualified individuals to the IT manager for a detailed interview. Let's start by looking at techniques for evaluating the job history of a networking professional.

Evaluating Employment History

Evaluation of a network administrator job candidate's work history is the single most critical factor in résumé screening. Candidates without significant work history may spend an undue amount of time learning their jobs, while a more expensive, experienced candidate may be a better overall value for the hiring company.

Not all networking experience is equal. Many demanding IT shops provide excellent training and experience, while others provide only glancing exposure to advanced networking issues.

When evaluating network administrator work experience, the following factors need to be considered:

Network Administrator job role – Candidates who have had positions of responsibility within their organization are often more qualified than those candidates for whom the network administrator skills were a part-time duty.

Employer-sponsored Network Administrator education - Many large corporations require yearly training for all IT employees, and on-the-job education is a clear indicator of the employer's quality. Employer-sponsored, yearly training and participation in groups and conferences (Networld+Interop, Cisco Networkers) are indications of a good background for a networking professional.

Fraudulent Work History

In the soft market of the early twenty-first century, it is not uncommon for a desperate network administrator job applicant to forge a work history with a defunct dot-com. The desperate applicant hopes that this fraud will not be detected. This phenomenon presents the IT manager with a unique challenge in verifying employment history with a company that no longer exists or contacting job references that cannot speak English.

In many cases, the HR staff strongly discounts résumés where the employment and educational history cannot be completely verified. Many departments, frustrated with confirming overseas employment histories, never forward these types of résumés to the IT manager.

Evaluating Personal Integrity

It is always a good idea to perform a background check, which is easily obtained via national services. Many companies require that a candidate not have any criminal convictions, except minor traffic violations. In some cases, a routine background check can reveal arrests and acts of moral turpitude.

A network administrator professional's ongoing responsibilities often include securing mission-critical applications and confidential data. Therefore, some companies require that all applicants for networking positions be expected to demonstrate the highest degree of personal and moral integrity.

In addition, acts of moral turpitude, such as a history of drug use, dishonesty, lying, cheating, or theft may be grounds for immediate rejection. In some companies, all applicants are expected to sign a waiver to disclose personal information and are asked to submit to a polygraph exam.

Evaluating Academic History

While formal education is not always a predictor of success at a networking administration job, there can be no doubt that job candidates with advanced degrees from respected universities possess both the high intelligence and persistence needed in a top-notch networking professional.

The Quality of Education

When evaluating the educational background of job candidates, it is important to remember that not all colleges are created equal. Many IT managers tend to select candidates from top tier colleges and universities because they rely on the universities to do the prescreening for them.

For example, an IT professional who has been able to enroll in a top tier university clearly demonstrates high achievement, high intelligence, and a very strong work ethic. At the other end of the spectrum, there are many IT candidates who have attended vocational schools, night schools, and non-accredited universities to receive bachelor's degrees in nontraditional study areas. In many cases, these IT professionals lack the necessary technical and communicational skills required to succeed in the IT industry.

Hardware networking skills may be desirable.

The type of degree is also a factor in the suitability of the IT candidate. For example, an ABS or MS in Computer Science generally requires the IT job candidate to have a very strong theoretical background in mathematics and physics. Those with formal degrees in computer science tend to gravitate toward software engineering and software development fields that require in-depth knowledge about lower-level components in computer systems.

On the other hand, we see the Bachelor's and Master's degrees in Information Systems. Those degrees offered by accredited business colleges (accredited by the American Assembly of Collegiate Business Schools, AACBS) tend to strike a balance between IT programming skills and business skills. The information systems degree candidate will have a background in systems analysis and design, as well as familiarity with functional program development for specific business processes.

Unlike computer science majors, information systems majors will have a background in accounting, finance, marketing, economics, and other areas of business administration that equip them to solve business problems.

Many IT shops save time by letting universities pre-screen networking professional candidates. For example, MIT carefully screens grades and achievement, and this pre-screening by the university allows companies to choose computer science professionals with increased confidence in the candidate's required skills.

Note: This section is based upon the author's experience in evaluating networking professionals and the HR policies of large IT shops. This section is in no way meant to discredit those network administrator job applicants without the benefit of a college education.

Rating College Education

Many shops have an HR professional evaluate the validity of the candidate's education, while other IT managers take it upon themselves to evaluate the quality of the network administrator candidate's formal education. Fortunately, sources for rating colleges and universities can be found online. Many large corporations require that the job candidate's degree must be from a university possessing a first-tier or second-tier rating by US News & World Report's "America's Best Colleges" or degrees from exceptional universities (as listed in the Gourman Report).

Of course, not all networking jobs require a college degree. For lower-level networking jobs, the formal academic requirements are less challenging, but the lead network administrator for a large corporation must possess high intelligence, superb communications skills, and the drive and persistence that is most commonly associated with someone who has taken the time to invest in a quality education.

College Major and Network Administrator Job Suitability

There is a great deal of debate about what academic majors, if any, are the best indicators of success in a networking professional position. However, it is well documented that different majors attract students with varying abilities. The following list describes some indicators used in large corporations for assessing the relative value of different college majors:

Engineers - Engineers tend to make great networking professionals, especially those with degrees in Electrical Engineering (EE). An engineering curriculum teaches logical thinking and data structure theory that make it easy for the engineer to learn networking quickly. However, while engineers have unimpeachable technical skills, their oral and written communication skills are often lacking. Therefore, IT managers should pay careful attention to communication skills when interviewing applicants with engineering degrees.

Business Majors - Business majors make excellent network administrators because of their training in finance, accounting, marketing, and other business processes. Many business schools also require matriculated students to take several courses in information technology. Not all college business schools are equal, though. When screening a network administrator job applicant with a business major, time should be taken to insure that the degree is from a business school accredited by the American Assembly of Collegiate Business Schools (AACSB). There are many fly-by-night business schools, and their depth of training may be vastly different.

Computer Science Majors - Computer scientists typically receive four years of extensive technical training, and are ideal candidates for network administrator jobs requiring in-depth technical ability. However, like the engineers, many computer scientists have sub-standard communications skills.

Music Majors - For many years, IBM recruited from the ranks of college musicians because hiring managers found that musicians possessed an ability in logical thinking that made them ideal candidates for IT skill training.

Math Majors - Math majors tend to possess excellent logical thinking skills and often possess a background in computer science. Like many quantitative majors, social and communications skills may be a concern.

Education Majors - Evaluation of education majors is extremely difficult because of the wide variation in quality between universities. Nationally, GRE test rankings by academic major show that education majors consistently rank in the lowest 25% of knowledge. Any applicant with an education major should be carefully screened for technical skills, and the college ranking checked in US News & World Report's "America's Best Colleges".

Some network administrators are insecure about their vocabulary

International Degrees

A huge variation in quality exists among international degrees. Therefore, Network Administrator professional candidates with international degrees should be carefully checked in the "Gourman Report" of International Colleges and Universities.

Some sub-standard overseas colleges have no entrance requirements and require little effort from the student. There has also been a rash of résumé falsifications of college degrees from overseas colleges.

"Yes, I was an NCAA Basketball All-star"

Some job candidate may lie!

The fraudulent applicant is often relying upon the human resource department's inability to successfully contact the overseas school to verify the applicant's degree.

In sum, international degrees should be carefully evaluated. It is recommended that, where appropriate, foreign language professionals are hired to write the letters to request verification of the graduate's attendance, and to obtain and translate the college transcript.

Advanced Degrees and Network Administrator Professionals

Approximately 30% of the network administrators for large corporations possess an advanced degree (Masters or Doctorate). While an advanced degree shows dedication to a professional position, the quality of the degree is of paramount concern.

A higher ranking should be given to an on-site master's degree from a respected university than to a night school or "non-traditional" graduate school. These non-traditional schools often have far lower acceptance standards for students and are far less academically demanding than the top US graduate programs.

"I've been a CCNA for 35 years."

The New Graduate

Regardless of the educational experience of the graduate, there will likely be little in his/her background that will prepare him/her for the real-world business environment. Computer curricula tend to emphasize theoretical issues of interest to academicians that may have little direct bearing on the needs of your shop.

New College graduates are sometimes immature.

Your company will need someone who can work within the existing IT system without crashing and burning the edifice down. The work that the new employee does on the system will be modified and altered by others in the future, as new needs develop and hidden problem areas emerge. For this reason, a candidate who is able to show the technical interviewer that he has excellent documentation skills and habits can be a tremendous asset to the company over someone who is not accustomed to submitting work that must be accessible to others. Several of the questions in Chapter 5 are useful for gauging these traits.

Personality of the Network Administrator

What is more important to managers, technical knowledge or personality? Many times, managers concentrate too much on technical skill, and a candidate's personality is overlooked.

Some Network Admins have split personalities.

In almost every core network administrator job function mentioned above, the network administrator's work is made up of interacting with vendors, users, developers, and managers. With that in mind, the following professional personality traits are, or ought to be, embodied by the successful network administrator.

For some Network Administrators, everything is an emergency!

These traits are important for people in almost any profession, but they are particularly important for network administrators. Let it be said of the successful networking professional that he or she is self-confident, curious, tenacious, polite, motivated, and a stickler for details.

Self-confidence

Network administrators that lack self-confidence, ask the manager's opinion on every decision no matter how large or small, and show no initiative, are not all-star material. This indecision may be acceptable for a new network administrator working under the supervision of a senior network administrator, but the network administrator must learn to depend on his or her own judgment for important decisions.

Some Network Administrators don't take initiative.

In interviews, questions must be asked about problems encountered and how the applicant would resolve the problems. Answers provided should reflect self-confidence.

A Curious Nature

Curiosity is a core trait of the network administrator because the network is constantly changing, and those changes are not always documented. A network administrator who is not curious is passive and reactive, while a curious network administrator is proactive.

A self-aware Net Admin sees reality clearly.

The curious network administrator invests personal money to stay current. In interviews with potential network administrators, questions should be asked about the books and subscriptions the candidate relies upon. Needless to say, answers indicating sole reliance on "the documentation set" are not an indication of professional curiosity.

A Tenacious Disposition

Like most disciplines in the IT industry, bulldog-like tenacity is required for troubleshooting as a network administrator. The network administrator should enjoy knuckling down on a problem and not giving up until an answer is found.

Polite Manners

A network administrator works closely with other people. Therefore, tact is required when dealing with developers, managers, and users.

But, here's a fact of the network administrator's life. Project managers, developers, and users will bring forth unreasonable requests and impossible deadlines. Interpersonal skills must be cultivated by the network administrator to respond to such requests without burning bridges. Ill-will is fostered outside the IT department by a rude network administrator. They must be extra polite, beginning in the job interview.

Some Network Administrators have a reputation for poor manners!

Self-Motivating

Employers value self-starting employees who require little supervision. Twice as much self-motivation is expected from the network administrator than other IT professionals, primarily because the network administrator must often take charge of critical projects. In addition, successful network administrators prevent fires before they start, and smart network administrators know what things can cause trouble if they are ignored.

Personal motivation is a major factor in successful Network Administration.

Detail Oriented

Being detail-oriented is perhaps the most important trait for a network administrator. Network administrators are often described as having an "anal" personality, after Sigmund Freud's theory of anal-retentive personalities. A good networking professional should not have to be told to crosscheck details or to document quirks observed during an installation.

Attention to Detail is critical for Network debugging.

A detail-oriented person is early for an appointment and brings a PDA or calendar to an interview. Questions asked by the detail-oriented person are reflections of the research conducted about the potential new employer.

Conclusion

This chapter has been concerned with the specific criteria for evaluating work and academic history, and personality characteristics of applicants. Next, let's look at the roles of network administrators and get more insight into the desired traits of a successful network administrator.

Network
Administrator Roles

A good network administrator candidate is able to articulate a solid knowledge of techniques in all areas of networking, including installation, configuration management, security, monitoring and tuning, and troubleshooting. In addition, a successful network administrator professional in any organization must also possess above average communication skills.

Network Administrator Job Roles

The job of network administrator means many things to many people. What the new network administrator does is determined by the size of the employer. In a small shop, the network administrator's duties are much broader than in corporations with teams of networking professionals dedicated to specific projects.

Is the employer doing development? Is it utilizing third party packages? The functions of the network administrator position are also determined by the answers to those questions. The interviewee and the interviewer must be prepared to discuss and understand what is expected of the network administrator and the role of the network administrator within the company hierarchy.

User Management - The network administrator is responsible for enrolling users and maintaining system security.

Disaster Recovery - A key duty of the network administrator is to develop and maintain disaster recovery plans, working closely with the systems and other IT staff to ensure the company is able to operate in the event of an emergency.

Hardware Management – Maintenance and upgrades to the internetworking devices and network infrastructure are performed by the network administrator.

Network Administrator and End-user Liaison - In contacting vendors for technical support, the network administrator becomes the official company representative and contact point for the vendor.

To sum up, a full-charge network administrator candidate is knowledgeable in installation, configuration management, security, monitoring and tuning techniques, backup and recovery strategies, vendor relations, and of course, troubleshooting.

Let's drill-down and review the basic knowledge areas for the network administrator candidate.

Policy

Key to the smooth operation of a corporate network is a comprehensive set of policies. These policies not only benefit the IT staff, but the other employees as well. A good network administrator understands the importance that policy plays in a corporate environment, and can give examples of good policies designed to protect the company, its employees, and its data.

Documentation

A successful network administrator understands the critical role that documentation plays in any network strategy. Documentation should be kept up to date and reviewed often.

Security

Having a clear understanding of network security options is fundamental to the network administrator skill set. Knowledge of how to integrate operating system security options with the network is vital.

Monitoring and Tuning

Part of the network administrator's daily routine is monitoring and tuning the network. The network administrator's knowledge base must include detailed understanding of the network.

In interviewing for a network administrator position, candidates should be prepared to discuss their previous experiences with monitoring and tuning networks.

Troubleshooting

The flair for troubleshooting is a characteristic that is not common to all people. The art of troubleshooting requires an analytical approach, where the problem is laid out in discrete parts, and each is attacked in a methodical fashion until the problem can be resolved.

Troubleshooting sometimes requires the network administrator to admit he or she does not know something and must have the wherewithal to look for the answer. In responding to questions about troubleshooting, the network administrator candidate should be prepared to discuss real-life experiences. The best examples are those illustrating a lot of thought and multiple troubleshooting steps.

Communication Skills

Great technical skills are needed by the network administrator, but technical knowledge alone does not guarantee job success. As mentioned earlier, a network administrator needs to be polite when dealing with fellow professionals, managers, vendors, and end users. Because a significant percentage of the network administrator's work requires interacting with others on multiple levels, network administrators must be able to speak, think, and write clearly and concisely. A network administrator should strive to set the standard for quality oral and written communication skills.

An inventory of a network administrator's communication skills starts with the professional résumé. A network administrator's résumé should be easy to read and reflect the candidate's publishing and speaking credits. Whether the network administrator was a keynote speaker at a national conference or merely presented a topic at a local user group, those experiences document the candidate's communication skills.

The interviewer should bring questions about job experiences that required the candidate to write documentation or procedures. It should be assumed that candidates with an advanced degree, such as a Masters' or PhD, have well-developed writing skills, or they would not have reached that level of education. Candidates are encouraged to bring to the interview their dissertations or other writing samples.

A successful network administrator absolutely must possess strong verbal communication skills. The ability to listen is just as important as the ability to speak clearly. The professional Network Administrator's daily routine will include listening to complaints and requests, processing that information, and providing responses and instructions.

Conclusion

The network administrator professional must have a well-rounded skill set, and not just technical skills. Next, let's explore screening techniques for networking professionals and examine techniques and tools for verifying technical skill.

Initial Screening

Preparation

Significant amounts of money and resources can be saved by thoroughly preparing and paying close attention to details during the screening process. Additionally it could also prevent potentially disastrous problems from ever occurring. Filling vacant positions is expensive, and a careful approach during the initial screening can reap tremendous dividends over time.

Any Network Administrator who is fluent in Klingon may have a personality disorder.

In the opinion of many network managers, an effective network administrator should have plenty of significant rcal-world experience to supplement technical knowledge. In many large corporations, the network administrator is a respected technical guru who participates in all phases of system development, from the initial system analysis to the final physical implementation. Hence, the network administrator generally has significant experience in development, systems analysis, and systems administration.

The High Cost of Attrition and Hiring Overhead

The IT industry suffers from one of the highest attrition rates of all professional jobs. This is due, in part, to the dynamic nature of changing technology, where a job candidate may find himself grossly underpaid and decide to market his skills within a relatively short period of time. The high attrition rate is also due to the lack of challenge within many IT shops that can occur after the job candidate has become successful in their work.

For example, an IT job candidate might enter a shop that needs a great deal of work, only to stabilize the environment to the point where they tend to be bored most of the time. The IT manager must try to distinguish between the "job hopper" and the individual who is changing jobs solely because of a personal need for more challenging work.

The cost of hiring varies by position and by geographic location, but is rarely less than $10,000 per employee. Filling higher end positions, such as senior network administrator or database administrator, can often exceed $50,000, as specialized headhunters are required in order to locate the candidate. These headhunters commonly charge up to 50 percent of the candidate's first year wages for a successful placement. There are also the fixed costs of performing background checks and credit checks, as well as HR overhead incurred in checking the individual's transcripts and other résumé information.

Choosing Viable Candidates

While reviewing hundreds of applications for a single job, the IT manager must quickly weed-out "posers" and job candidates who do not know their own limitations. To be efficient, the network manager must quickly drill-down and identify the best three candidates to invite for an in-depth technical interview by an experienced network administrator.

Shops that do not have a current network administrator generally hire a network administrator consultant for this task.

Nit-picky Network Admins document everything!

Network administrator consultants are commonly asked to help companies find the best network administrator for a permanent position. Later on, we show some of the questions used when evaluating network administrator candidates for corporate clients.

Dealing with IT Headhunters

When seeking a top-level IT position such as senior database administrator, database architect, or chief of network security, it is not uncommon to employ IT headhunters. These IT headhunters can charge up to 50 percent of the IT job's base salary in return for a successful placement.

However, the aggressive nature of the IT headhunters often does a disservice to the IT candidate, and puts the IT manager in a tenuous position. For example, it is not uncommon for the IT manager to receive résumés from two different sources for the same candidate, each represented by different firms. In cases like this, it is prudent to immediately remove that candidate from the prospective pool, in order to avoid the inevitable feuding between the competing headhunter firms.

When dealing with headhunters, it's also important to get a guarantee that the IT employee will remain in the shop for a period of at least one year and to amortize the payments to the headhunter over that period. Those IT managers who fail to do this may find themselves spending up to $50,000 for a job candidate who quits within ninety days because they are not satisfied with their new job.

It's also important to remember to negotiate the rate with the headhunters. While they may typically command anywhere between 25 and 50 percent of the IT employee's first year gross wages, these terms can indeed be negotiated prior to extending an offer to the IT candidate. In many cases, this works to the disadvantage of the IT candidate, especially when the headhunter refuses to negotiate the terms, thereby making another candidate more financially suitable for the position.

General Evaluation Criteria

Remember, all networking professionals are not created equal. They range from the Network Administrator BS (Network Administrator Baby Sitter) level to a fully skilled, fire-breathing network administrator with extensive credentials. What level of network administrator professional does the company require? Consider what happens if a fire-breathing network administrator is employed in a position that requires only monitoring maintenance. That fire-breather will soon grow bored and find work elsewhere. On the other hand, hiring a Network Administrator BS for a slot that requires tenacity, drive, initiative, and top-shelf troubleshooting skills is begging for disappointment.

A good Network Administrator is always available!

It is not easy to match the right candidate for a given job. Given the choice between someone who could re-write TCP/IP from scratch (but lacked certain personality skills) and a technically inexperienced network administrator professional who demonstrates the personality traits mentioned above, the less experienced candidate is frequently the best choice.

The typical Network Administrator Baby Sitter usually has a good-looking résumé that is full of projects and jobs involving network administration. However, the interviewer must subtract points if that work involved existing setups and the Network Administrator's main duties were monitoring. When the candidate can't answer in-depth questions concerning the networks they have worked with in the past, the person is a Network Administrator BS candidate.

High scores should be given to candidates who have direct knowledge of common networking utilities, such as packet sniffers and intrusion detection systems.

A rule of thumb for hiring network administrators is to avoid hiring an overqualified person who won't be happy in a job with minimal responsibilities. In a shop that utilizes a third-party monitoring tool a Network Administrator BS who can jump into gear whenever the tool identifies a problem should be hired.

On the other hand, if a full-charge network administrator is needed, a newbie Network Administrator BS should not be hired, unless the newbie clearly demonstrates the motivation for high-end learning and the desire to become a full-fledged network administrator.

You can always tell a successful CCNA.

Gleaning Demographics from the Candidate

With the affirmative action laws in the United States, the IT manager must be careful never to ask any questions that are inappropriate or illegal. For example, asking the marital status, the number and age of the children, or the age of the applicant himself may make the IT manager vulnerable to age and sex discrimination lawsuits. Hence, the savvy IT manager learns to ask "safe" questions that still reveal the information, while protecting the manager and company from lawsuits.

Don't wind-up in court over an illegal interview question!

While the IT manager certainly does not want to discriminate against the job applicant, the demographical aspects of the job applicant nevertheless factor strongly into the hiring decision. For example, the female job applicant who has three children less than five years of age may not be appropriate for an IT position that requires long hours on evenings and weekends.

Another example is age. If the IT manager works for a company that guarantees retirement where age plus years of service equals 70, then hiring a 60-year-old candidate would expose the company to paying that candidate a lifetime pension for only a few years of service.

Elderly Network Engineers can add spice to the workplace!

Other important demographical information in our highly mobile society is the depth of connection the IT candidate has to the community. Those IT candidates who do not have extended family, close relatives, and long-term relationships in the community may be tempted to leave the position in order to seek more lucrative opportunities in other geographical areas.

Given that this information is critical to the hiring decision and at the same time inappropriate to ask directly, the savvy IT manager may ask somewhat ambiguous questions in order to get this information. For example, the manager may ask "What do you do to relax"? This open-ended question will often prompt the candidate to talk about activities they engage in with their families and with the community.

Be sure to screen for mental health issues!

Generally, the selection of a network administration professional can be accomplished through the following phases:

1. Initial screening of résumés by the HR department (keyword scan)

2. Non-technical screening by the IT manager (telephone interview)

3. In-depth technical assessment by a senior network administrator

4. On-site interview (check demeanor, personality, and attitude)

5. Background check (verify employment, education, certification)

6. Written job offer

Résumé Evaluation

As mentioned, it is not uncommon to receive hundreds of résumés for a particular networking job. The goal of the IT manager (or HR department) is to filter through this mountain of résumés and identify the most-qualified network administrator candidates for the job interview.

You cannot always identify drug users

The HR department typically performs a quick filtering through a large stack of résumés in order to narrow the candidates down to a select few, which are in turn presented to the IT manager.

Some résumés may contain anomalies that can reduce the time required for screening. These résumé anomalies are known as "red flags", and indicate that the job candidate might not be appropriate for the IT position. These indicators can quickly weed out dozens of candidates, eliminating the need for a more detailed analysis of the résumé, saving company resources.

Résumé Red Flags

There are several important things to look at when scanning a stack of résumés. The following is a short list that is used by many IT managers:

- **Unconventional résumé formatting and font** - Occasionally you may see a nice résumé that is done in a professional font, with elaborate graphics, sometimes even including photographs and illustrations. In extreme cases, résumés have been known to arrive printed on pink paper scented with expensive perfumes.

- **Too much information in the résumé** - Another red flag is a résumé that tends to specify a great deal of non-technical information. For example, the job candidate may go into great detail about their love of certain sports, hobbies, or religious and social activities. In many cases, these résumés indicate an individual for whom the IT profession is not a great priority.

- **Puffing insignificant achievements** - It is not uncommon for low end IT positions to attract job candidates who will exaggerate the importance of trivial training. For example, an IT job candidate may proudly list on his résumé that he attended classes on how to use Microsoft Word in the work environment. Of course, trivia within an otherwise nice résumé too often indicates a lack of real technical skill, and the job candidate may be making an effort to obfuscate that fact by simply listing anything that they can think of.

- **Gaps in employment time** - It's important to understand that the technically competent IT professional is always in demand and rarely has any kind of gaps in their employment history. Sometimes, IT professionals misrepresent their work chronology in their résumés. For example, if they are laid off and are job seeking for 90 days, they may not list that ninety-day gap of unemployment in order to make themselves seem more attractive. Of course, the start and end dates of each term of employment must be carefully checked by the HR department, and any false indication of this should be grounds for immediate removal from the candidate pool.

- **Poor grammar and sentence structure** - Because the IT industry tends to focus more on technical than verbal skills, you may often find candidates with exceptional technical skills but whose poor writing ability is clearly apparent on their résumés.

Short, choppy sentences, incorrect use of verbs, and misspellings can often give you a very good idea of the candidate's ability to communicate effectively via e-mail. Remember, the résumé is a carefully crafted and reviewed document. If you find errors in this, you're likely to hire a candidate who lacks adequate written communicative skills.

- **Short employment periods** - Within the IT industry, it is very rare to be dismissed from a position in less than six months. Even the incompetent IT worker is generally given 90 days before they're put on probation and another 90 days before they are dismissed from the job. Hence, an immediate red flag would be any IT employee whose résumé indicates that they've worked with an employer for less than 6 elapsed months.

Evaluating Training

Scanning résumés involves two factors: evaluation of work history and academic qualifications. Here are some criteria that have been used by major corporations for résumé screening.

Network administrator job candidates used to have only two sources for networking knowledge: experience and/or vendor certification classes. Experience speaks for itself and can be judged as to depth and level of experience. However, any training is only as good as what the candidate puts into the training.

In other words, the candidate could either gain much or comparatively little from the experience of certification training, depending on whether they took their "will to learn" and curiosity with them to class.

Troubleshooting skills are essential for the Network Administrator.

As we have noted, Cisco certification (offered by Cisco Systems, Inc.) is one benchmark of a modicum of competence. The

CCNA and CCNP exams test the candidate's knowledge in all areas of the professional skill set.

In order to pass, a candidate will, in almost all cases, need to have had actual experience as a network administrator and will need to have knowledge from multiple networking references. While obtaining a Cisco certification is no absolute guarantee that a candidate is fully qualified, it can be used as an acid test to separate the wheat from the chaff.

Telephone Screening

After reviewing the available résumés, you will be in a position to select a pool of candidates for further telephone screening. The telephone interview is a useful tool for weeding those candidates whose actual qualities may not quite match their glowing résumés, saving considerable time and expense over on-site interviews.

The telephone is your best tool for pre-screening technical skills.

The interview may be either unscheduled or prearranged. In both cases, the candidate will be less prepared than for the more formal on-site interview, and it can quickly become apparent whether that candidate is a good choice to fill the position.

The unscheduled telephone screening is an opportunity to discover how well the candidate thinks on his feet, and provides insight into his unrehearsed thoughts and feelings. It can also indicate how well the candidate is organized, since the person who has to repeatedly search for basic necessary materials and documents at home is unlikely to demonstrate superior efficiency in the work environment.

The interviewer should cover all pertinent areas, with the goal of confirming the qualifications presented in the résumé. The candidate should be well-informed about those topics which the résumé indicates are areas of proficiency.

The telephone interview will also reveal a great deal about non-technical qualifications. Is the candidate personable and articulate? How well do they listen?

The information and impressions gathered from the telephone screening will enable the IT manager to confidently select the best-qualified candidates for an in-depth technical interview.

Technical Pre-Testing

The job interview questions in this text are deliberately intended to be presented orally. While these questions often help determine a candidate's level of experience and skill with a specific technology, many IT managers will require the job candidate to take an in-depth technical examination.

The technical examination may be given over the internet, using job testing sites such as Brain Bench, or they may be paper and pencil tests administered to the candidate before the start of a detailed job interview.

There are important legal ramifications for the use of these testing methods. Many job candidates who are not selected for an important position may challenge both the scope and validity of the test itself. These challenges have been applied even to nationally-known aptitude tests such as the SAT and LSAT exams; IT exams and language tests, such as C++, may be especially prone to challenge by the disgruntled IT professional.

While it is important to do a complete check of all the technical abilities of the IT candidate, it is very important for the IT manager never to cite the failure of one of these exams as the reason for removal from the applicant pool. This is a common technique used by IT managers when they find a particular candidate's knowledge of the field to be insufficient.

For example, in a highly competitive IT vacancy, very small things may wind up making the difference. In any case, when rejecting a candidate, the IT manager should generally cite something intangible, such as the job skills do not completely meet the requirements of the position, or a more nebulous answer, such as the candidate's interpersonal skills will not mesh with the team environment. Remember, specific citation of failure of any tangible IT testing metric may open your company to challenges and lawsuits.

Developing Questions for Interviews

Interview questions should be diligently researched and the expected answers listed prior to the interview. Where open-ended questions are used, the interviewer should have the level of knowledge required to judge the correctness of the answers given by the candidate.

- The questions should be broken into categories and each should be assigned a point value based on either a scale, such as from 0-5 or according to difficulty. Technically competent personnel should review interview questions for accuracy and applicability.

- At the conclusion of the interview, evaluation of technical ability should be based on the results from these points.

In addition, "open-ended" questions should be included, such as "Describe the most challenging problem you have solved to date", or "Name one item that you have developed that you are most proud of". These open-ended questions are designed to allow the network administrator job candidate to articulate and demonstrate their communications skills.

The IT Candidate's Demeanor

During the face-to-face interview, the IT manager can glean a great deal about the personality of the individual simply by observing his/her body language and listening to the candidate speak.

"My long-term career goal?
Actually, I want to get your job."

In many cases, the IT manager may base the assessment of the interview candidate on non-technical criteria, especially the behavior of the candidate when asked pointed questions. Some of these demeanor factors include:

Eye Contact

IT candidates who are unwilling or unable to maintain eye contact with the interviewer may not possess the interpersonal skills required to effectively communicate with end-users and co-workers.

Fidgeting

IT candidates who are experiencing high anxiety during an interview may cross and uncross their legs, sit uncomfortably, or twiddle their hair while speaking with the IT manager. These involuntary signs of discomfort may indicate that the candidate does not function well in the stressful environment of a busy IT shop.

Diction

For those IT positions that require exceptional communicative skills, such as working with the end-user community, you can get a very good idea of the abilities of the job candidates simply by listening to their responses. For example, careful IT professionals may demonstrate the "lawyer's pause" before answering the question. This pause, of about two seconds, often indicates that the job candidate is thinking carefully and formulating his response before speaking.

Job candidates who formulate their answers carefully can be especially useful in those positions where the risk of damage from impulsive verbal statements, without considering the consequences of the statement, is high. You can also assess how articulate the job candidate is by the use of filler words such as "you know", inappropriate pauses, poor diction structure, poor choice of words, and a limited vocabulary.

Appropriate Appearance

A network administrator job candidate who doesn't take the time to put the right foot forward by maintaining a proper appearance probably doesn't have the wherewithal to perform adequately in the job. Clean, appropriate clothing and proper grooming show that the candidate is willing to make the effort to please the employer. Candidates who are sloppy in appearance and mannerisms will bring those characteristics to the job and to their interactions with other parts of the company.

Make sure your Network Administrator understands proper dress codes.

Savvy network administrator professionals will adopt the dress of the executive and banking industry. This attire generally includes:

- Crisp white shirt

- Conservative tie

- Dark suit

Dark leather shoes

Proper job interview attire is important.

We will take a closer look at the on-site interview in the next chapter.

Conducting the Network Administrator Job Interview

Conducting the Background Check

As we have repeatedly noted, a candidate's references must always be rigorously checked. Previous employers should be spoken with, if possible, to learn about a candidate's past work history. Many people are good at interviewing but won't necessarily function in the job.

Because of the explosive growth of the IT industry, fraudulent résumés have become increasingly common. Job candidates have been known to fabricate their college educations and the scope of their work experience, smooth over gaps in their employment history, and exaggerate their job skills. In some cases, job skills may be exaggerated inadvertently, because the job candidate has only a brief exposure to a technology and does not understand their own limitations.

"Yes, I know Cisco, TCP/IP, and two other Network words."

Therefore, it is very important for the HR department to perform a complete résumé check before forwarding any of these candidates for detailed interviews by the IT manager. These background checks may require the candidate's waiver signature for the release of all medical, criminal, and credit-related records.

The high rate of fraud found in résumé applications has spawned a new industry of private investigators, who for a fixed fee, will check national databases, revealing any criminal activity on the part of the job candidate, a history of bad credit, and other moral and demographic factors that may be relevant to their suitability for the position.

Making the Initial Job Offer

Once the IT manager has chosen the first candidate, it is common to make an offer based on nation-wide studies of the average salaries within the geographical area. For example, IT professionals in expensive, professional urban areas, such as New York City, will earn twice as much as an IT professional with the same skills, working in a cheaper suburban or rural area.

If you decide to make an offer to a candidate, it is a good idea to ask them the salary amount they have in mind. If the candidate is the first to mention a number, the company is placed in an advantageous negotiating position.

If the candidate indicates he will be satisfied with an amount that is lower than you were prepared to offer, then you have arrived at the ideal hiring scenario. You have a candidate that you have already decided is desirable for the position, and they will take less money than you had anticipated paying them.

On the other hand, if the candidate has an unreasonably high expectation given his skill level and the market in your area, he may have an unrealistic view of the current business environment. This can indicate either that the candidate didn't do his homework or simple wishful thinking. You might point out that the range for this position is somewhat lower than he anticipates. You can then offer the amount you originally had in mind, and negotiate from there.

The savvy IT manager will try to offer a candidate with an excellent set of IT skills a balance between the "going rate" and other intangible benefits, in order to make the job appealing. Other intangibles might include additional vacation time, flextime, telecommuting, additional vacation days, and other perks designed to make the job more attractive to the candidates.

Of course, the IT manager may deliberately reduce the size of the initial offer if he anticipates that the candidate may negotiate for more. A highly desirable IT candidate may be courted by multiple companies and will often respond to the job offer with a counteroffer, citing other employers who are willing to pay more for the same skill set. When this happens, the IT manager may soon be faced with the dilemma of paying more than they desired for the candidate, and may also question the candidate's motive in earning a high salary.

Conclusion

In sum, while the recession of 2002 has created a shakeout within the lower ranks of networking professionals, IT managers remain committed to retaining their top network administrator talent, and those network administrator professionals with specialized skills are still in high demand.

In today's highly volatile work environment, the average network administrator professional rarely stays with a single employer for a long period of time. Competition remains extremely strong for those network administrator superstars whose skill and background make them indispensable. While some attrition is inevitable, there are many techniques that savvy IT managers can use to retain their top talent.

At this point, you should be ready to invite the candidate for an on-site interview. Let's look at an approach to conducting a technical interview to access the candidate's level of technical knowledge.

The On-site Interview

During the on-site interview, the network administrator professional needs to be evaluated for both technical skills and non-technical personality traits that will indicate whether the candidate can be successful in the work environment.

Now it's your turn to ask the tough questions!

The specific areas that you choose to emphasize in the interview will depend on the nature of the position. A project manager who coordinates the efforts of several people will need a different skill set than someone who primarily works only with data. Choose questions that will highlight the specific skills you need and look for past experiences that demonstrate those abilities.

An effective IT manager must be able to wear many hats. He must have the creative vision necessary for planning projects, the interpersonal skills involved in communicating with a project team and coordinating their efforts, and he must serve as a liaison between upper management and the people who implement the project. Ask questions that demonstrate these abilities and look for experiences that show accomplishments in these areas.

Questions from the Candidate

Most books and articles neglect to discuss the questions that the candidate may ask the interviewer. This is unfortunate, because whether or not the candidate asks questions, and the character of those questions, can reveal a lot about his personality and suitability for the job.

After all, the serious candidate is evaluating the company just as you are evaluating him. If he is able to ask intelligent questions that are intended to assess how well his particular abilities and goals will integrate with the job, he is actually doing part of your job for you.

A certain amount of nervousness is inherent to the interview process, but the passive candidate who appears reluctant or unable to answer interview questions, as if under cross-examination, can only raise suspicions about the reason for his reticence. Contrast this person with the engaging candidate who doesn't answer so much as he conversationally responds, volunteering the pertinent information while interspersing his responses with questions of his own.

The candidate's questions should focus on the tasks and responsibilities he will encounter in the performance of his job. If the candidate takes the initiative in this way, facilitating the interview as you mutually explore whether the position is a good fit, chances are he will bring this same constructive approach to the work environment once you determine that he is, indeed, the best person for the job.

Beware the candidate who only seems to be interested in his salary and the other perks that he will enjoy. There will be time to discuss money once you both decide that the alliance between you is promising. The thrust of the interview should be on the requirements of the position and whether the candidate is equipped to meet them.

Technical Questions

The following questions were developed in case no one in your organization is qualified to assess the job candidate's skill set. Even without detailed knowledge of network administration, you can get a vague idea of the technical skills of your network administrator job candidate.

While this quick technical check can be administered over the telephone, it is often performed on-site by a certified and experienced network administrator. Each question is unambiguous with a clear answer.

The interviewer should begin by apologizing for asking pointed technical questions before reading each question verbatim. If a candidate asks for clarification or says that he or she does not understand the question, the interviewer re-reads the question. If the candidate fails to answer a question or answers incorrectly, the interviewer should respond "OK," and move immediately to the next question.

Not all Network Administrators have equal intelligence.

IMPORTANT NOTE:

The intention of this section is not to provide a comprehensive technical exam, and the technical questions in the code depot are only intended to be examples. The only way to accurately evaluate the technical skills of a job applicant is to employ the services of an experienced person and conduct an in-depth technical interview and skills assessment.

Also note that the expected answers from the questions are highly dependent upon the version of the product and the candidates' interpretation of the question. We have tried to make the questions as version neutral as possible, but each new release of every product brings hundreds of changes and new features, and these example questions may not be appropriate for your version. An experienced technical person should always administer the interview questions presented in this book.

Qualifications

1. Do you have any Certifications? (i.e., Cisco, Microsoft, CISSP)

   Answer: _____

   Comment: _____

2. Highest level of education?

   Requires a college education, preferably a BS in computer science or related engineering field.

   Answer: _____

   Comment: _____

Cisco questions

Cisco has been the largest and most successful vendor of internet working products for many years. The ability to work with Cisco equipment has become a prerequisite for today's network administrator. The questions here should indicate whether the candidate possesses Cisco knowledge concurrent with the Cisco Certified Networking Associate certification.

1. In the Cisco IOS, what mode must you be in to set the hostname on a router? How do you enter that mode from the initial router interface?

   Skill level: Intermediate

   Expected answer: To change this global setting, you must be in global configuration mode. To enter global configuration mode, you must first enter privileged exec mode by typing 'enable' and then entering the enable password. You then type 'config term' to enter global configuration mode.

2. In the Cisco IOS, what command will display the current running configuration of the router?

   Skill level: Low

   Expected answer: show running-config

3. What commands would you type in the Cisco IOS to set the IP address on the first Ethernet interface to 192.168.1.10/24?

   Skill level: Intermediate

   Expected answer:
   ```
   Router> enable
   Router# config term
   Router(config)# int e0
   Router(config-if)# ip address 192.168.1.10 255.255.255.0
   ```

```
Router(config-if)# exit
Router(config)# exit
Router# copy run start
```

4. What UDP-based protocol is used to upgrade the IOS of a Cisco router over a network?

   Skill level: Low

   Expected answer: TFTP (Trivial File Transfer Protocol)

5. What are the commands necessary to enable the IGRP routing protocol on a Cisco router and make it a member of autonomous system number 100? The router is directly connected to the class C networks 192.168.1.0 and 192.168.10.0.

   Skill level: High

   Expected answer:

```
Router> enable
Router# config term
Router(config)# router igrp 100
Router(config-router)# network 192.168.1.0
Router(config-router)# network 192.168.10.0
Router(config-router)# exit
Router(config)# exit
Router# copy run start
```

6. In the Cisco IOS, what command is used to display the IP routing table? What mode must you be in to issue this command?

   Skill level: Intermediate

   Expected answer: In privileged exec mode, the command is 'show ip route'.

7. In the Cisco IOS, what commands would be necessary to create an access control list that would block any telnet attempts from the internet to the router itself or any system

behind the router? Assume that the router's internet interface is s0.

Skill level: High

Expected answer:

```
Router> enable
Router# config term
Router(config)# ip access-list 101 deny tcp any any eq
telnet
Router(config)# ip access-list 101 permit any any
Router(config)# int s0
Router(config-if)# ip access-group 101 in
Router(config-if)# exit
Router(config)# exit
Router# copy run start
```

8. There are 6 types of Access Control Lists that can be created on a Cisco router. List these 6 types and the number range associated with each.

Skill level: High

Expected answer:

Protocol	Range
IP	1-99
Extended IP	100-199
AppleTalk	600-699
IPX	800-899
Extended IPX	900-999
IPX Service Advertising Protocol	1000-1099

9. On a Cisco router, what does the command 'show cdp neighbors' do?

Skill level: Intermediate

Expected answer: CDP is an acronym for Cisco Discovery Protocol. This is a proprietary Cisco protocol that is used to identify other Cisco devices on a network. 'show cdp neighbors' will list the other Cisco devices that are directly connected to the router, giving details such as:

- Device ID

- Local interface

- Platform

- Port ID

10. Define and describe a VLAN.

   Skill level: Intermediate

   Expected answer: VLAN is an acronym for Virtual Local Area Network. A VLAN is a group of hosts on a network segregated by software as opposed to hardware. A single switch can host multiple VLANs, and when systems need to communicate with systems outside their VLAN, they must first go through a router.

   VLANs give you the ability to segment your network logically, and to change that segmentation through software, without moving switches or cables.

Physical and Data-Link layer questions

1. What is a MAC address?

   Skill level: Low

   Expected answer: The MAC (Media Access Control) address is a unique 48-bit number assigned to every device that will communicate on an Ethernet network. The number is separated into two parts: the first 24 bits assigned to a vendor and the last 24 bits uniquely identifying the device.

2. What are the advantages fiber offers over copper in network wiring?

   Skill level: Intermediate

   Expected answer: Fiber is not subject to electrical interference. Unboosted fiber can be pulled much farther than copper cable. While Category 5 UTP copper cable can only run 100m unboosted, multi-mode fiber is rated to 2000m and single-mode fiber to 5000m.

3. Why is it important to main twists to within no less than 1/2" from a punch down panel when working with Category 5 UTP?

   Skill level: Low

   Expected answer: The twists in Category 5 Unshielded Twisted Pair greatly reduce the electrical interference in the wire itself, and also reduce the chance of crosstalk.

4. What are the specifications that govern the correct wiring of Category 5 copper cable?

   Skill level: Intermediate

   Expected answer: EIA/TIA-568A and EIA/TIA-568B

---

5. What switching protocol is used to prevent network loops in a Layer 2 network?

Skill level: Low

Expected answer: Spanning Tree Protocol (STP)

6. How does a member of an IP network determine the MAC address of another member in the same subnet?

Skill level: Low

Expected answer: ARP (Address Resolution Protocol) Request

7. How does a member of an IP network determine the MAC address of a system on a different subnet?

Skill level: Low

Expected answer: It doesn't. A host will never know the MAC address of another host on a different subnet. MAC addresses are only required for layer 2 communications, and communicating across subnets is layer 3 communication.

8. Why is it desirable to use switches instead of hubs in an Ethernet LAN environment?

Skill level: Low

Expected answer: Switches will create more collision domains, reducing the amount of systems that will be affected by a collision. This segmenting at Layer 2 allows for greater efficiency and throughput.

9. What is a DLCI?

Skill level: High

Expected answer: DLCI (Data Link Connection Identifier) is a number that identifies the logical circuit associated with the endpoints of a frame relay connection.

10. Define and describe the two authentication methods that are available with a PPP connection.

    Skill level: High

    Expected answer:

    PAP (Password Authentication Protocol) is the less secure authentication method, because it only authenticates at the beginning of the conversation, making it susceptible to a man-in-the-middle attack.

    CHAP (Challenge Authentication Protocol) is the more secure, as it will periodically reauthenticate the sender with a challenge/response mechanism.

11. Define and describe a CSU/DSU.

    Skill level: Intermediate

    Expected answer: A CSU/DSU (Channel Service Unit/Data Service Unit) is a device used to connect a local area network to a wide area network. This device normally exists between the router on a LAN and the demarcation point of the WAN, converting the LAN signaling and frame types to WAN signaling and frame types.

12. What is the difference between a circuit-switched and a packet-switched network?

    Skill level: Intermediate

    Expected answer: A circuit switched network consists of connection oriented virtual links where traffic is usually predictable and relatively constant. Circuit switched networks are common for voice communications. A packet switched network consists of different networks connected by many varying paths. The dynamic nature of a packet switched network increases the reliability of the data, but can cause latency issues. The multiple paths inherent in a packet switched network also make for more 'bursty' data patterns. Packets switched networks are commonly used for data communications.

13. What is WEP?

Skill level: Intermediate

Expected answer: WEP (Wired Equivalent Privacy) is the encryption available in 802.11b LANs. A WEP key can be 64 or 128 bits. Unfortunately, due to a poor implementation in 802.11b, WEP keys are relatively easy to recover with freely available tools.

14. Describe the current wireless LAN standards, and discuss the pros and cons of each.

Skill level: High

Expected answer:

- 802.11b is rated for speeds up to 11 Mbps and operates in the 2.4GHz band. 802.11b devices are cheap and plentiful, but their relatively slow speeds and poor WEP implementation make them a poor choice for enterprise business use.

- 802.11g is rated for speeds up to 54 Mbps and operates in the 2.4GHz band. 802.11g fixes the speed problems experienced with 802.11b while still remaining backward compatible. However, the 2.4GHz band is already crowded with many other non-regulated signals, making troubleshooting difficult.

- 802.11a is rated for speeds up to 54 Mbps and operates in the 5GHz band. 802.11a operates in the less used 5GHz band, making it easier to co-exist with other wireless devices. The lack of backward compatibility with 802.11b devices has slowed its adoption in the consumer market.

15. In a Layer 2 switch, what is the difference between cut-through and store-and-forward switching?

Skill level: High

Expected answer: Cut-through switching will examine a data frame as it comes in the originating interface. As soon as the destination of the frame is determined, the switch begins forwarding the frame to the destination port. This fast handling of a frame reduces latency (the time the frame spends inside the switch) at the cost of reliability (no checksum is performed on the frame.) Store-and-forward switching will wait until the entire frame has been read from the originating interface. A checksum will then be verified, ensuring the integrity of the frame. The frame is then forwarded to the destination interface. This switching mode is more reliable, but increases latency.

16. Define and describe FDM and TDM.

Skill level: High

Expected answer:

- FDM (Frequency Division Multiplexing) is a way to combine many signals on the same communications channel. These signals are separated by assigning each one a unique frequency, or subchannel, within the main channel.

- TDM (Time Division Multiplexing) is also a way to combine many signals on the same communications channel. However, in this case, the signals are separated by breaking each signal into many smaller segments, which are then reassembled at the destination based on timing of the signals.

Both of these technologies require the use of a multiplexer to combine the signals at the transmitting end.

Security Questions

Security, always an important part of network administration, has gained much publicity in the last few years, as network attacks have become more prevalent and more publicized. The important thing to look for when interviewing a network administrator candidate is their attitude towards security. Practical knowledge is important, of course, but the truly high level network administrator understands that security is a process, not a product. Security must permeate everything that happens on the network, from adding and removing hosts to troubleshooting routing problems. Only by placing security as the number one priority will the network administrator be able to ensure the reliability and availability of the network. Specifically, their response to question 11 will give great insights into what role security plays in their idea of a network.

1. What issues are involved with operating a packet sniffer on a switched Ethernet network?

   Skill level: Intermediate

   Expected answer: Since a system connected to a switched Ethernet network will only see traffic originating from it, destined for it, or broadcast traffic, a packet sniffer isn't as useful as it is on a shared Ethernet network. In order to utilize a sniffer to its fullest potential, you must designate a port on one of the backbone switches as a management port. This will instruct the switch to copy all traffic to this port, regardless of the source or destination address. When you connect your packet sniffer to this port, all Ethernet traffic will be seen.

2. You have a Cisco router connecting your LAN to the Internet and you are utilizing the built in firewall capabilities of the

Cisco IOS. If a packet traverses your firewall rules and does not match any of them, how does the IOS treat that packet?

Skill level: Intermediate

Expected answer: The Cisco IOS will drop the packet. Cisco always implements an "implicit deny" after all firewall rules, meaning that any packet not matching any rule is dropped. In order to reverse this behavior, you must have a firewall rule (normally the last one) that implicitly allows a packet.

3. Discuss the pros and cons of stateless and stateful firewalls.

    Skill level: High

    Expected answer:

    - Stateless firewalls require much less overhead, and introduce less latency into the network. They examine each packet individually, with no thought to the packet's relationship to other packets.

    - Stateful firewalls will take into account the fact that a packet is part of a larger data "conversation," and can make better decisions on what traffic to allow or deny. This comes at the cost of added complexity in setup and greater latency in the network.

4. What is source-address verification, and why is it an important part of firewall implementation?

    Skill level: Intermediate

    Expected answer: Source-address verification is the process of monitoring all outbound data at a network endpoint, and only allowing data out of the network if the source address matches the subnet from which the data originated. This effectively eliminates "source address spoofing," a common tactic used in denial of service attacks when an attacker is attempting to mask the source of their packets. If this kind of egress filtering was done on all networks on the internet, the amount of denial of service attacks would be greatly reduced.

5. What is a DMZ and why is it important?

   Skill level: Low

   Expected answer: DMZ stands for "demilitarized zone." It is a term borrowed from the military that refers to a separate network setup between a company's private network and the public internet. If a company needs to allow internet access to a service, that service will run on a host in the DMZ. This 'buffer zone' is desirable because if a system in the DMZ is compromised, an attacker still has no access to the company's private network.

6. Define and describe a VPN.

   Skill level: Low

   Expected answer: VPN stands for Virtual Private Network. Using encryption software, it is possible to setup a secure, encrypted 'tunnel' between two points on a public network (like the internet). Once this link is established, those two points form a virtual private network, allowing secure communication to take place over an insecure medium.

7. Define and describe the two main types of VPNs in use on the internet today.

   Skill level: Intermediate

   Expected answer: PPTP VPNs are based on the Point-to-Point Tunneling Protocol. This protocol is backed by a coalition of vendors, headed by Microsoft. Client and server software packages to implement this VPN solution are included with versions of Windows after Windows 98 OSR2.

IPSec based VPNs are commonly implemented in hardware VPN solutions from companies like Cisco. IPsec supports two security schemes: Authentication Header (AH), which authenticates the sender of the data; and Encapsulating Security Payload (ESP), which supports sender authentication and payload encryption.

8. Define the private IPv4 subnets, and explain their importance to the security of a network.

   Skill level: Intermediate

   Expected answer: In order to allow for easy adoption of TCP/IP inside corporate networks, without the possibility of address conflict with the internet, private IP subnets were created. These ranges of IP addresses are non-routable, meaning they are not valid on the internet.

   - Class A private IP range: 10.0.0.0 – 10.255.255.255
   - Class B private IP range: 172.16.0.0 – 172.31.0.0
   - Class C private IP range: 192.168.0.0 – 192.168.255.255

   Adopting a private IP address space is recommended for a corporate network. This prevents any system on the internet from directly addressing any internal system. Internal systems are granted outside access by means of Network Address Translation or a proxy server.

9. Define NAT and describe the benefits.

   Skill level: Low

   Expected answer: NAT (Network Address Translation) is used most often in conjunction with a private IP subnet, a system running NAT will forward packets from one network to another, making all source packets appear as if they originate from the NAT system itself. When a reply is received, the reverse happens, with the NAT system rewriting the destination address to allow the packet to be delivered to the requester. This proxying of packets is an important security practice. It also allows a large number of systems to access an outside network through a single IP address.

10. Describe SSL and trusted third-party Certificate Authorities.

Skill level: High

Expected answer: SSL (Secure Sockets Layer) was developed by Netscape to address the insecurities of HTTP communication. SSL is a protocol that allows for the encryption of HTTP sessions using key-based cryptography.

On the internet, there is little in place to prove that someone is who they say they are. Just because you can make an encrypted connection to someone's online web store, that doesn't mean that they are a legitimate business. The business of Certificate Authorities has arisen to aid in authenticating these transactions. When a business purchases a certificate from a trusted Certificate Authority (like Verisign or Thawte Consulting), that certificate is presented to every web browser that attempts to make a secure connection to the business' web site. If the web browser trusts the third party Certificate Authority, the connection is allowed. If not, the connection is denied. A list of the major Certificate Authorities is included with the major web browsers. The analogy for this connection is "I don't trust you, but I trust Verisign, and they tell me that you are who you say you are."

11. What is the weakest point in every network?

Skill level: Intermediate

Expected answer: People. Regardless of how good your firewall, intrusion detection systems, audits and personnel are, your employees will always be the weakest link in your network.

Social engineering is a common way to attempt to exploit the people in a networking environment. Why should a cracker spend days attempting a brute force attack to discover a password, when he can call up a secretary, impersonate someone from the IT department, and get her to give him her password?

Every security policy should include basic security principals for every employee, such as:

- Never give your password out over the phone or in email

- Challenge any suspicious person you see in the office, etc.

12. What is a smurf attack, and how can it be prevented?

Skill level: High

Expected answer: A smurf attack is a term for a common denial of service attack utilizing ICMP packets. An attacker will craft an ICMP echo packet appearing to originate from the victim's IP address. This packet will be sent to the broadcast address of another network. Since packets sent to a broadcast address are accepted by every system on a subnet, and since the standard response to an echo request is an echo reply, the victim soon finds his IP address flooded with ICMP echo replies from this network.

The recommended way to thwart this kind of attack is to block access to broadcast addresses at each network's router.

13. What is a SYN flood, and how can it be prevented?

   Skill level: High

   Expected answer: All TCP connections begin with a three-way handshake. This handshake consists of a SYN from the source, a SYN-ACK reply from the destination, and an ACK from the source. When a system receives a SYN packet, it allocates memory space to handle the connection, sends the SYN-ACK, and waits for the final ACK before communication can occur. This is what is known as a half-open connection.

   A SYN flood occurs when an attacker sends a large amount of SYN requests to a system, spoofing the source IP address of the packets. This will cause the victim's system to send SYN-ACKs to systems that weren't expecting them, and will therefore not reply. As the spoofed packets continue to come in, the victim's system will continue to allocate memory to handle these half-open connections until eventually the memory of the system is exhausted and no more incoming connections are accepted.

   There is currently no generally accepted solution for handling this kind of problem because it utilizes the very nature of TCP communication as opposed to exploiting vulnerability. The recommended solution is for originating networks to perform source-address verification on all outgoing packets, eliminating the possibility of a system on their network sending out packets with spoofed IP addresses.

TCP/IP and Routing questions

Because TCP/IP is the routing protocol in use on the internet, it has become the protocol of choice for most corporate LANs as well. The understanding of how TCP/IP operates is critical for a network administrator, as the majority of the network troubleshooting they will be faced with will involve TCP/IP.

1. RIP is a common, simple routing protocol. What metrics does RIP use to determine the path a packet should take?

   Skill level: Low

   Expected answer: Hop count.

2. What is the difference between a routing protocol and a routed protocol?

   Skill level: Intermediate

   Expected answer: A routing protocol is used by routers to exchange information about the networks to which they are connected. Examples of routing protocols are RIP and IGRP.

   A routed protocol is a communications protocol that can be routed. A protocol can only be routed if it uses a hierarchical addressing scheme. Examples of protocols that can be routed are TCP/IP, IPX, and Appletalk.

3. System A has the IP address 192.168.5.41 and a subnet mask of 255.255.255.248. What are the network address and broadcast address of System A's subnet?

   Skill level: Intermediate

   Expected answer: Network Address is 192.168.5.40. Broadcast Address is 192.168.5.47

4. How many usable IP addresses are there in a subnet that is created by taking a class C subnet and adding a subnet mask of 255.255.255.252?

Skill level: Intermediate

Expected answer: 62 usable IP addresses (64 total, minus the network and broadcast addresses)

5. What separates IGRP from the simpler routing protocol RIP?

Skill level: High

Expected answer: A router using IGRP uses an autonomous network number to identify the networks to which it is connected. IGRP takes into account more metrics than RIP, including bandwidth, delay, load, reliability, and maximum transmission unit (MTU).

6. Examine the following routing table:

```
Destination Gateway     Genmask        Flags Metric Ref Use Iface
192.168.2.0 0.0.0.0     255.255.255.0  U     0      0   0   eth0
10.1.1.0    10.1.1.1    255.255.255.0  U     0      0   0   eth1
127.0.0.0   0.0.0.0     255.0.0.0      U     0      0   0   lo
0.0.0.0     192.168.2.1 0.0.0.0        UG    0      0   0   eth0
```

If a packet originated with this system, and was destined for 10.1.1.10, by which interface would it travel?

Skill level: High

Expected answer: Interface eth1. Since 10.1.1.10 is in the network described by the static route for 10.1.1.0, the second routing table entry applies.

7. Why is the initial TCP connection between two systems known as a 'three-way handshake'?

Skill level: High

Expected answer: When System A wants to initiate a TCP connection with System B, it first sends a SYN packet to System B (this is the first part of the handshake). System B replies with an ACK, and sends a SYN of its own (this is the second part of the handshake). System A replies with an ACK (this is the third part of the handshake) and TCP data can now be sent between the two systems.

8. How many TCP and UDP ports numbers are there? What are the three assigned ranges?

   Skill level: High

   Expected answer: There are 65535 TCP and UDP port numbers (2 to the 16th power).

   - 0 – 255 are reserved for public applications.

   - 256 – 1023 are available to companies for commercial networking applications.

   - 1024 – 65535 are unregulated.

9. Define and describe CIDR.

   Skill level: High

   Expected answer: CIDR (Classless Inter-Domain Routing) is also referred to as *supernetting*. CIDR gives us the ability to segment a network farther than the standard Class A, B, and C subnets defined by IPv4. By subnetting these networks, a company wishing to add 300 hosts to a network does not have to jump from a class C (254 hosts) to a class B (65,533 hosts).

   CIDR network addresses look like this: 192.168.1.0/24

   The 24 means that the first 24 bits of the IP address are the network part of the address, leaving 8 bits for the host part.

10. What are the TCP applications associated with the following port numbers?

Skill level: Intermediate

Expected answer:

- TCP Port 80 : http
- TCP Port 25 : smtp
- TCP Port 22 : ssh
- TCP Port 20 : ftp-data
- TCP Port 21 : ftp
- TCP Port 23 : telnet
- TCP Port 110 : pop-3
- TCP Port 143 : imap

Telephone pre-interview questions

1. What are the seven layers of the OSI Networking model?

   Expected answer:

   - Physical
   - Data-Link
   - Network
   - Transport
   - Session
   - Presentation
   - Application

2. How many bits are there in an IPv4 address?

   Expected answer: 32 bits

3. Category 5 Unshielded Twisted Pair (UTP) cable is rated for how many meters without a repeater?

   Expected answer: 100 meters

4. What program is used to display the route between two hosts on a TCP/IP network?

   Expected answer:

   - traceroute (Unix)
   - tracert (DOS and Windows)

5. What protocol does the ping command employ to determine the availability of hosts on a TCP/IP network?

   Expected answer: ICMP (Internet Control Message Protocol)

6. In an IP subnet, what two IP addresses can you not assign to hosts?

   Expected answer: The network address and the broadcast address

7. What is the default subnet for a Class C IP subnet?

   Expected answer: 255.255.255.0 or /24

8. What does the acronym VPN stand for?

   Expected answer: Virtual Private Network

9. What are the two switching types employed in a Layer-2 switch?

   Expected answer: Store and forward & Cut-Through

10. CSMA/CD is commonly used to describe the capabilities of an Ethernet. What does CSMA/CD stand for?

    Expected answer: Carrier Sense Multiple Access / Collision Detection

Troubleshooting Questions

The most important skill a network administrator must possess is the ability to troubleshoot problems. A good troubleshooter not only understands the technologies involved in the problem, but also has the ability to think logically and to break down a problem into smaller parts, establishing control variables that can be easily tested. The answer given for the first question in this section will tell you a lot about your network administrator candidate.

1. A user contacts you and tells you that she cannot access any web sites. All you know about the network setup is that the workstations are TCP/IP hosts on a switched Ethernet network, and they connect to the internet through a DSL line. What are the steps you take to diagnose the problem?

   This is the most important question you will ask the candidate. The most important skill a network administrator possesses is the ability to diagnose and logically dissect a problem. There are many different ways to solve this problem, but in this case you're looking for how the candidate answers the question as opposed to what their answer is. A skilled network administrator will break the problem down, eventually isolating the issue through deductive reasoning and process of elimination. The ordering of the process is important as well. When troubleshooting a networking issue, you must always begin at the lowest level and work your way up.

   Skill level: Low – High

   Expected answer: Here is a sample response that indicates a good approach to identifying the problem. The candidate should give a similar answer. This will indicate the candidate understands the processes involved and the order in which to troubleshoot them:

- First, we must verify the physical connection to the network. Is there an Ethernet cable connected to the Ethernet card in the computer? Is there a link light on the connection?

- Next, verify the correct addressing and protocols are in use. Does the computer have an IP address? Is it a valid IP address for the subnet in which they reside? Is the subnet mask correct? Is the default gateway correct? Is the primary DNS server correct?

- Next, start the standard network troubleshooting tests. Can you ping the loopback address? Can you ping the default route? Can you contact the primary DNS server? Is it responding to queries?

- Next, verify the application level settings. Does the user go through a proxy server or other caching server to access the internet? If so, is there authentication involved?

- Finally, verify the scope of the problem. Is this problem unique to this machine or this user? Does anyone else in the department or subnet have the same problem?

- As you can see, there are many paths to take to identify this problem, but someone who displays a logical, thorough understanding of the steps involved will be able to identify the problem within a reasonable amount of time.

2. You issue a ping command on a TCP/IP network, and receive the following response:

```
$ ping 192.168.1.250
PING 192.168.1.250 (192.168.1.250) 56(84) bytes of data.
From 192.168.1.1 icmp_seq=1 Destination Host Unreachable
```

What does this response mean?

Skill level: Low

Expected answer: This response indicates that the originating computer believes it knows the correct route to connect to 192.168.1.250, but it did not receive a reply back from the destination system. Most likely, the 192.168.1.250 system is offline. You can also tell by this response that 192.168.1.1 is the default gateway of this subnet.

3. You issue a ping command on a TCP/IP network, and receive the following response:

```
$ ping 192.168.1.250
PING : Network is unreachable
```

Skill level: Low

Expected answer: This response indicates that your host is not currently participating on the IP network. This is often an indication that your host does not have an IP address assigned to it.

4. You issue a ping command an a TCP/IP network, and receive the following response:

```
$ ping 192.168.1.250
PING 192.168.1.250 (192.168.1.250) 56(84) bytes of data.
64 bytes from 192.168.1.250: icmp_seq=1 ttl=128 time=0.6 ms
64 bytes from 192.168.1.250: icmp_seq=1 ttl=128 time=0.6 ms (DUP!)
```

Skill level: Intermediate

Expected answer: This response indicates that there are two hosts on the network responding to queries for 192.168.1.250.

5. The traceroute command is used to display the hops between two hosts on a TCP/IP network. Explain why it is sometimes possible to access a web site using HTTP but still be unable to traceroute to it?

Skill level: Intermediate

Expected answer: The traceroute program uses ICMP (Internet Control Messaging Protocol) packets to do its job. If a router or host is blocking ICMP, traceroute will fail but other protocols (like HTTP) will work. Also, traceroute depends upon the fact that each router in the hop list will reply to the sender with a "Time Exceeded" message. Not all routers support this, and some can be configured to not answer traceroute queries in this manner. So while traceroute can be an important network troubleshooting tool, you cannot rely on it as your only indicator of connectivity.

6. You have a laptop with an 802.11b wireless network card installed. You are near a wireless access point, yet you cannot make a connection. What things do you need to verify in order to establish a connection?

Skill level: Intermediate

Expected answer: In order to be a member of a wireless network, you must ensure the following three things:

- You know the SSID of the network you wish to join

- If WEP encryption is being used, you must have a valid key

- Your signal must be strong enough (this is dependent upon your physical proximity to the access point and the amount of interference in the band you are using)

7. You have a computer with the IP address of 1.1.1.10. This computer is connected to an Ethernet hub. Also connected to this hub is the first Ethernet interface on a router. The interface on this router has an IP address of 1.1.1.1. The second interface on this router is plugged into a second hub,

and has the IP address of 2.2.2.1. Connected to the second hub is a computer with an IP address of 2.2.2.10. Describe the settings that are required in order for the two computers to communicate with each other using TCP/IP.

Skill level: High

Expected answer: The first computer must have a subnet mask that matches the subnet mask assigned to the first Ethernet interface on the router. The first computer must have the IP address of the first Ethernet interface on the router as its default gateway, and it must be able to ping that address. The same is true for the second system. It must be in the same subnet as the second Ethernet interface on the router It must have the IP address of the second Ethernet interface on the router as its default gateway, and it must be able to ping that address. Finally, the router itself must be configured to pass packets between these two Ethernet interfaces. This is accomplished by either a static route or by enabling a routing protocol such as RIP on the router.

8. What will this command do?

```
tcpdump -i eth0 icmp
```

Skill level: Intermediate

Expected answer: This command will display all of the ICMP packets seen on the eth0 interface.

9. Two computers are connected to a hub with Ethernet cable. Computer A has an IP address of 192.168.1.1 and a subnet mask of 255.255.255.0. Computer B has an IP address of 192.168.2.1 and a subnet mask of 255.255.255.0. Can these two computers communicate over TCP/IP? Why or why not?

Skill level: Low

Expected answer: No. Because these computers are in different subnets, they would need a router between them in order to communicate.

10. Two Cisco routers are connected by a DCE/DTE cable. Serial0 on Router1 is the DCE and Serial1 on Router2 is the DTE. Both interfaces are assigned IP addresses in the same subnet, and the subnet mask reflects this. However, no data can currently pass between these interfaces, and the 'show int s0' and 'show int s1' commands say that the line protocol is down on both interfaces. What needs to happen before this link can be brought up?

Skill level: Intermediate

Expected answer: Because this is a point-to-point WAN connection, a clock rate must be negotiated before communication can occur. Since Serial0 on Router1 is the DCE, the clock rate must be set there. The following commands must be issued on Router1:

```
Router1> enable
Router1# config t
Router1(config)# int s0
Router1(config-if)# clock rate 56000
```

Note: The 56000 should reflect the preferred clock rate.

Non-Technical Questions

When conducting an on-site or telephone interview, it's very important that you be able to assess non-technical information about your job candidate. These non-technical factors include motivation, thinking skills, and personal attitude. All of these factors have a direct bearing on the ultimate success of the candidate in your shop. They also give you an idea about the potential longevity of a particular candidate.

Each of these questions is deliberately ambiguous and probing so that the job candidate will have an opportunity to speak freely. Often these questions will give you a very good idea of the suitability of the candidate for the position. Remember, in many IT shops technical ability is secondary to the ability of the candidate to function as a team member within the organization.

1. What are your plans if you don't get this job?

    This question can reveal a great deal about the motivation of the job candidate. If the candidate indicates that he/she will change career fields, going into an unrelated position, then this person may not have a long-term motivation to stay within the IT industry. If, on the other hand, the candidate responds that he will continue to pursue opportunities within the specific technical area, then the candidate is probably dedicated to the job for which he is being interviewed.

2. How do you feel about overtime?

    This is an especially loaded question, because any honest job candidate is going to tell you that they don't like to work overtime. As we know, the reality of today's IT world is that the professional will occasionally have to work evenings and weekends. This question is essential if you're interviewing for a position that requires non-traditional hours, such as a network administrator or database administrator, where the bulk of the production changes will occur on evenings, weekends, and holidays.

3. Describe your biggest non-technical flaw.

This question provides insight into the personality of the job candidate, as well as their honesty and candor. Responses are unpredictable and may range from "I don't suffer fools gladly" to "I have difficulty thinking after I've been on the job for 16 hours". Again, there is no right or wrong answer to this question, but it may indicate how well the candidate is going to function during critical moments. More importantly, this question gives an idea of the level of self-awareness of the candidate and gauges whether or not they are actively working to improve their non-technical skills.

4. Describe your least favorite boss or professor.

The answer to this question will reveal the candidate's opinions and attitudes about being supervised by others. While there is no correct response to this question, it can shed a great deal of light on the candidate's interpersonal skills.

5. Where do you plan to be ten years from now?

This is an especially important question for the IT job candidate because it reveals a lot about their motivations. As we know, the IT job industry does not have a lot of room for advancement within the technical arena, and someone who plans to rise within the IT organization will be required to move into management at some point. It's interesting that the response to this question is often made to be overly important, especially amongst those managers that hear the response "in ten years I would like to have your job."

6. How important is money to you?

Again, this is an extremely misleading question, because even though many IT professionals deeply enjoy their jobs, and some would even do it for free, money is a primary motivator for people in the workplace. This question provides an easy opportunity to find out whether or not your candidate is being honest with you.

An appropriate answer for the candidate might be to say that he greatly enjoys his work within IT but that he needs to be able to maintain some level of income in order to support his family. A bonus benefit of this question is it also provides insight into the demographic structure of the job candidate, namely their marital status, as well as the age of their children, and whether or not they have immediate family in the area. It is well known within the IT industry that job candidates are most likely to remain with the company if they have a large extended family group within the immediate area

7. Why did you leave your last job?

This is one of the most loaded questions of all, and one that can be extremely revealing about the personality of the IT job candidate. The most appropriate answer to this question is that the previous job was not technically challenging enough, or that the candidate was bored.

However, periodically you will find job candidates who will express negativity regarding the work environment, the quality of the management, and the personalities of the co-workers. This of course, should be a major red flag because it may indicate that this job candidate does not possess the interpersonal skills required to succeed in a team environment.

8. If you were a vegetable, what vegetable would you be?

On its face, this is a totally ludicrous and ambiguous question, but it gives you an opportunity to assess the creative thinking skills of the job candidate. For example, if the job candidate merely replies "I don't know", he may not possess the necessary creative thinking skills required for a systems analyst or developer position.

A creative candidate will simply pick a vegetable, and describe in detail why that particular vegetable suits their personality. For example, the job candidate might say "I would be broccoli because I am health-oriented, have a bushy head, and go well with Chinese food."

9. Describe the month of June.

The answer to this question also provides insight into the thinking ability of the job candidate. For example, most job candidates may reply that June is a summer month, with longer days, hot weather, and an ideal vacation time. The candidate with an engineering or scientific point of view might reply instead that June is a month with 30 days that immediately precedes the summer equinox.

10. Why do you want to work here?

This is the candidate's opportunity to express why he might be a good fit for your particular organization. It also indicates whether the candidate has taken the time to research the company and the work environment. Is the candidate applying for this position solely because he needs a job, any job, or because he has specifically singled out your company due to some appealing characteristic of the work environment?

This question can also add information about the motivation of the job candidate, because a job candidate who is highly motivated to work for a particular firm will make the effort to research the company, the work environment, and even the backgrounds of individual managers.

Using a powerful search engine such as Google, the savvy IT candidate can quickly glean information about the person who is interviewing them. Having detailed knowledge of the organization is a very positive indicator that the candidate has given a lot of thought to the particular position and is evidence of high motivation.

General Questions

1. What do you know about our company?

   Answer: _____

   Comment: _____

   If the prospective employee has little or no knowledge about the company, then he will also have little idea about how he can benefit the company. A candidate who has not gone to the trouble of researching the organization may be after a job, any job.

   A candidate who has taken the time to explore the company will probably have specific ideas in mind about what he can bring to the organization. The initiative required by the candidate to research the company is a good sign that he is proactive and not passive dead weight.

   If the candidate has some knowledge of the company's mission and function, this will also become apparent in the questions he asks you. He will already be thinking about how he can fit in and how his skills can be utilized. These are desirable traits of a problem-solver.

2. Why do you want to work for this company? Why should we hire you?

   Answer: _____

   Comment: _____

   The answer to this question can reveal whether the candidate is merely shopping for a job or has true interest in the company and the position. It is important that the candidate show some passion for the field. If he does not, he will probably never be creative in the work environment and he will not represent a solution for you.

Does the candidate have a core belief that his particular set of skills can benefit you? Answers such as "I believe my experience can make a difference here," or "I believe your company will provide an environment that more directly engages my interest," or "Working for your company will provide challenges that excite me" are good starters.

3. Why are you looking for a new job?

Answer: _____

Comment: _____

Typical reasons for seeking a new job include the desire to advance in the field and boredom in a job that offers few fresh challenges. These are positive motivations, but there can be negative ones as well. There may be personal conflicts between the candidate and other team members or management that have become so adversarial that the candidate is compelled to leave.

While not necessarily eliminating a candidate from consideration, personal friction in the previous job does raise a red flag. It may be that the candidate is an unfortunate victim of backroom politics. However, if he confides in you regarding the shortcomings of his supervisors or fellow employees while taking no responsibility himself, consider yourself warned.

4. Tell us about yourself or your background.

Answer: _____

Comment: _____

This is probably asked more than any other question in interviews. It is the main opportunity for the candidate to describe his experiences, motivations, and vision of himself as it relates to the company.

The candidate should provide clear examples of how his abilities were used in the past to solve problems. If the candidate just repeats the information in the résumé, he is probably only going through the motions and has no clear vision of his role in the company.

Even worse, if the candidate contradicts the résumé, there is evidence of a serious problem.

5. What are three major characteristics that you bring to the job?

Answer: _____

Comment: _____

The candidate should offer specific skills or traits that he believes will be useful in the position. If the candidate is unable to relate these characteristics to the job, he has obviously not thought much about his role in the organization. You are interested in finding someone who has ideas about how he can hit the ground running and make a real difference to the company.

6. Describe the "ideal" job... the "ideal" supervisor.

Answer: _____

Comment: _____

This question is not as open-ended as it may seem. If the candidate's ideal job has little or nothing in common with the position he is interviewing for, he is unlikely to be a good fit. The candidate's response should match fairly well with the requirements of the position.

The candidate's description of the ideal supervisor can provide clues about how well the candidate works with superiors. Beware the candidate who seizes this as an opportunity to denigrate past managers.

7. How would you handle a tough customer?

Answer: _____

Comment: _____

Can the candidate provide examples of instances when difficult clients were won over? An effective communicator can strike a balance between meeting the needs of the customer and dealing with unrealistic expectations.

Above all, the candidate should indicate that he understands the necessity of "going the extra mile" to alleviate the concerns of the customer. Providing service to the client or end user is fundamental to the success of any enterprise.

8. How would you handle working with a difficult co-worker?

Answer: _____

Comment: _____

This is similar to the last question. The candidate should relate an example of a conflict with a co-worker or team member that was successfully resolved. What you are looking for is evidence that the candidate is able to facilitate communication and lead a difficult project to a successful conclusion.

9. When would you be available to start if you were selected?

Answer: _____

Comment: _____

10. How does this position match your career goals?

Answer: _____

Comment: _____

This is an excellent question to ascertain whether the candidate truly sees the position as an integral part of his career path. Does the candidate believe the knowledge and experience he will gain from this job will move him to where he wants to be?

A thorough answer to this question will lead into the next one.

11. What are your career goals (a) 3 years from now; (b) 10 years from now?

Answer: _____

Comment: _____

The answer to this question will indicate the level of commitment the candidate feels towards the job and the company. If the candidate has a goal in mind, how well does it fit with the job he is applying for?

When the candidate describes his goals, does he speak in terms of the skills and abilities he hopes to acquire that will prepare him for his eventual role, or does he simply want to be the CEO, with little thought of what it might take to get there?

The interviewer may be surprised by how often the candidate will talk about goals that are unrelated to the position.

12. What do you like to do in your spare time?

Answer: _____

Comment: _____

This question provides an opportunity to learn more about the character of the candidate, and to judge whether his outside interests complement his professional life. Is the candidate well-rounded or one-dimensional? Does he tend to sustain an interest over time?

13. What motivates you to do a good job?

Answer: _____

Comment: _____

If the candidate responds "making money" or "avoiding the wrath of my boss," you may have a problem. The candidate should describe some positive motivation, such as a new challenge, and tie it to a specific example of a time in the past when the motivation reaped personal rewards and results on the job.

14. What two or three things are most important to you at work?

Answer: _____

Comment: _____

The answer to this can reveal much about how the candidate sees himself on the job. Does the candidate mention things such as the importance of interpersonal communication, or responding quickly to crisis situations, things that facilitate job performance, or does he seem to be more worried about the timeliness of his coffee breaks?

15. What qualities do you think are essential to be successful in this kind of work?

Answer: _____

Comment: _____

Does the candidate have a realistic idea of what the work environment requires of him, and do the qualities of the candidate match the job? Does the candidate have an example of a past job experience when these qualities were called upon with beneficial results?

16. How does your previous work experience prepare you for this position?

Answer: _____

Comment: _____

This question is related to many of the others. If the candidate is able to articulate a clear idea of how his previous experience and training has prepared him for the responsibilities of the new position, he will be well ahead of many other interviewees.

17. How do you define "success?"

Answer: _____

Comment: _____

If the answer doesn't fit the position, the candidate may be unhappy in the field or quickly become bored. This indicates that the candidate may not be committed to staying with the company for very long.

18. What has been your most significant accomplishment to date?

Answer: _____

Comment: _____

The candidate should be able to relate a specific example of an achievement that demonstrates a desirable quality for the job. The candidate should focus on action and results, rather than long-winded descriptions of situations.

The answer to this question can provide insight into situations that the candidate may handle especially well. The candidate should demonstrate an ability to persevere and overcome obstacles. Did the person deliver more than was expected of him in a difficult situation?

19. Describe a failure and how you dealt with it.

Answer: _____

Comment: _____

This type of negative question can be extremely revealing. It can indicate significant weaknesses or problems that may interfere with the ability to do the job.

Was the failure a catastrophic one, or a relatively minor problem? Was the candidate able to learn from the experience and apply the knowledge to future situations?

The answer to this question can also reveal how much personal accountability and responsibility the candidate accepts. If the candidate blames the failure on others, he is not likely to learn from his mistakes.

As with most interview questions, this questions is designed to provide insight into the overall personality of the candidate, giving you a fuller appreciation of the strengths, as well as the weaknesses, of the person.

20. What leadership roles have you held?

Answer: _____

Comment: _____

This answer should indicate not only that the candidate has the leadership experience to succeed in the new job, but that he has the ability to work well with others and is able to shoulder the responsibility and deal with the pressure associated with the requirements of the position.

21. Are you willing to travel?

Answer: _____

Comment: _____

The answer here will demonstrate how committed to the company the candidate is likely to be. If the candidate dismisses the idea of travel completely, he may lack the motivation you are looking for.

22. What have you done in the past year to improve yourself?

Answer: _____

Comment: _____

This question can shed more light on the personality of the candidate. If the candidate has been motivated by the goal of obtaining this position, he will be able to demonstrate that he has taken the initiative to prepare himself for it.

If the candidate instead chooses to describe the benefits of his basket-weaving class, he may indeed be the better for it, but it has little relevance to solving the problems he would soon encounter in the new position.

23. In what areas do you feel you need further education and training to be successful?

Answer: _____

Comment: _____

If the answer has nothing to do with the offered position, the candidate may soon become bored. This question is similar to others and should dovetail with other answers about goals and career path.

24. What are your salary requirements?

Answer: _____

Comment: _____

If the candidate mentions a figure that is too low, he may be uninformed or desperate. On the other hand, if his financial expectations are unreasonable, he should probably be eliminated from consideration.

Policies, Processes and Procedures

The following questions are designed to zero in on key aspects of the candidate's personality and ability to perform. You may find it helpful to assign each response a score between 1 and 5 (a shorthand assessment technique that may also be used with many of the preceding questions).

You are trying to guage the candidate's ability to act in accordance with established guidelines, follow standard procedures in crisis situations, communicate and enforce organizational policies and procedures, and recognize and constructively conform to unwritten rules or practices.

1. On some jobs it is necessary to act strictly in accordance with policy. Give me an example when you were expected to act in accordance with policy even when it was not convenient. What did you do?

    Expected answer: Did the candidate follow policy because of commitment to it, even if a reason could be given for breaking it? Was there non-conformity to policy because of personal style, disrespect for those who made the policy, or revenge/dishonesty?

    Score: _____

    Comment: _____

2. What types of experience have you had in managing situations that involve potentially high money loss situations to ensure your job effectiveness?

    Expected answer: Did the candidate have a "no exceptions" strategy which showed systematic and rigorous use of policy and procedures to ensure consistency? Was there a dislike for rules and preferences to ensure consistency? Was there dislike for rules and preference for doing the job his/her own way?

Score: _____

Comment: _____

3. Describe a time when you found a policy or procedure challenging or difficult to adhere to. How did you handle it

Expected answer: Did the candidate take great pains to adhere to the policy and communicate the difficulty to proper management for review/revision? Was there an unnecessary risky deviation from policy, and no communication of either the challenge or deviation to management?

Score: _____

Comment: _____

Quality

The traits of a candidate who does quality work include their ability to maintain high standards despite pressing deadlines, establish high standards and measures, do work right the first time, inspect material for flaws, test new methods thoroughly, and reinforce excellence as a fundamental priority.

1. Describe a situation in which a crucial deadline was nearing, but you didn't want to compromise quality. How did you deal with it?

   Expected answer: Did the candidate maintain high quality through investing additional resources, moving deadlines, or making a statement of work in progress? Was there a quality sacrifice, possibly resulting in additional problems at a later time?

   Score: _____

   Comment: _____

2. Describe something you developed or coordinated that had to be exactly right. Exactly how did you test it?

   Expected answer: Did the candidate rigorously identify potential sources of problems, systematically address them, and run ample trails? Was there a brief accounting for possible problems, insufficient experimentation, or minimal piloting?

   Score: _____

   Comment: _____

3. Describe an effort you undertook to make product/service quality a fundamental priority in your business. Exactly what steps did you take to do this?

   Expected answer: Did the candidate implement training and error prevention/control/correction systems, or apply other systematic approaches? Was there a haphazard or inadequate support of quality functions?

   Score: _____

   Comment: _____

Commitment to Task

Commitment to task involves the ability to take responsibility for actions and outcomes and persist despite obstacles. To be available around the clock in case of emergency, give long hours to the job, demonstrate dependability in difficult circumstances, and show a sense of urgency about getting the job done.

1. Describe a difficult situation in which you took full responsibility for actions and outcomes. How did you act on this?

   Expected answer: Did the candidate publicly claim responsibility, and then carefully manage this situation to success, possibly one involving other parties with divergent goals? Was there allowance of others to accept blame, and little effort to resolve a difficult situation?

   Score: _____

   Comment: _____

2. Some people can be counted on to go the extra mile when their organization really needs it. Describe a time when you demonstrated dependability in trying circumstances.

   Expected answer: Did the candidate work long hours or perform unusual job duties to help the organization get through a personnel shortage, etc.? Was there minimal extra effort, consistent with the notion that it was the company's problem?

   Score: _____

   Comment: _____

3. Describe a time when you gave long hours to the job. For example, tell me about when you took work home, worked on weekends, or maintained long hours due to system maintenance.

   Expected answer: Did the candidate show self-direction and initiative in working particularly long hours, with clear dedication to a meaningful objective? Was there compliance to routine work requirements, possibly with resentment about what was expected?

   Score: _____

   Comment: _____

4. Give me an example of a time when you demonstrated a sense of urgency about getting results.

   Expected answer: Did the candidate take immediate action directed toward a specific objective, so that non-task activities and interests were given low priority while productivity and efficiency were of prime importance? Was there little emphasis on effectiveness/speed/efficiency?

   Score: _____

   Comment: _____

Planning, Prioritizing and Goal Setting

Your network administrator may be called upon to wear many different hats in this position. He/She should have the ability to prepare for emerging customer needs, manage multiple projects, and determine project urgency in a meaningful and practical way. Other desirable abilities include the ability to use goals to guide actions and create detailed action plans and the ability to organize and schedule people and tasks.

1. Describe a situation that illustrates how well you manage multiple projects simultaneously.

   Expected answer: Did the candidate keep all projects moving on a pace to hit deadlines and in a manageable, systematic, quality way, and using a meaningful approach to prioritizing? Was there haphazard allotment of resources to different tasks, with unproductive and unnecessary chaos?

   Score: _____

   Comment: _____

2. Priorities can be set meaningfully based on ease of task, customer size, deadlines, or a number of other factors. Describe a time when it was challenging for you to prioritize.

   Expected answer: Did the candidate use a sensible set or priorities and apply it consistently? Was there excess bouncing of resources, resulting in inefficiency, or a poor choice of criteria on which to prioritize?

   Score: _____

   Comment: _____

3. Think of a project in which you skillfully coordinated people, tasks, and schedules. How did you do it?

    Expected answer: Did the candidate use a systematic approach to identify tasks, people who can do the tasks, schedules, and constraints? Was there a simplistic approach that was inadequate given the complexities of the project?

    Score: _____

    Comment: _____

Attention to Detail

Attention to detail involves the ability to be alert in a high-risk environment, the ability to follow detailed procedures and ensure accuracy in documentation and data. Your network administrator may be called upon to carefully monitor gauges, instruments, or processes. He/She should be able to concentrate on routine work details and organize and maintain a system of records.

1. Describe a time when you had to apply changes to a mission critical system. What did you do to insure the stability of the system? What actions did you take and what were the results?

   Expected answer: Did the candidate dutifully monitor all potentially troublesome aspects of the environment, and address anything that seemed imperfect. Was there a casual awareness of potential trouble spots, and reliance on subsequent quick reactions rather than prevention?

   Score: _____

   Comment: _____

2. Select an experience from you past, which illustrates your ability to be attentive to detail when monitoring the systems environment. Tell me, in detail, what happened.

   Expected answer: Did the candidate show commitment to monitoring and understanding equipment and to using a strategy to ensure/enhance attention to detail? Was there little awareness of potential distractions, over-dependence on technology, or overconfidence?

   Score: _____

   Comment: _____

3. How have you gone about ensuring accuracy and consistency in a document or data you were preparing? Tell me about a specific case in which your attention to detail paid off.

   Expected answer: Did the candidate take clear precautions such as proofing thoroughly, double-checking, verifying format consistency, etc.? Was there only a cursory spot check?

   Score: _____

   Comment: _____

4. Tell me about your experience in dealing with routine work. What kinds of problems did you have to overcome in order to concentrate on the details of the job?

   Expected answer: Did the candidate use a strategy to maintain attentiveness during routine work? Was there acceptance of diminished alertness, with little effort being made to remove/reduce it?

   Score: _____

   Comment: _____

5. Give me an example that demonstrates your ability to organize and maintain a system of records.

   Expected answer: Did the candidate initiate or show commitment to a systematic method for organization or record keeping? Was there ineffective record keeping, overconfidence in memory, or dependence on others?

   Score: _____

   Comment: _____

Initiative

Initiative includes the ability to bring about great results from ordinary circumstances, prepare for problems or opportunities in advance, transform leads into productive business outcomes, undertake additional responsibilities, and respond to situations as they arise without supervision.

1. Tell me about a situation in which you aggressively capitalized on an opportunity and converted something ordinary into something special

   Expected answer: Did the candidate put a unique twist on a routine situation to yield unusually positive results, probably not achieved by others in similar situations? Was there an accomplishment of little magnitude or that should have been expected of anyone in that situation?

   Score: _____

   Comment: _____

2. Describe something you've done that shows how you can respond to situations as they arise without supervision.

   Expected answer: Did the candidate take reasonable and quick action with an appropriate amount of information or research, warranting the independence? Was there use of authority inappropriately, excess procrastination, or a bad decision?

   Score: _____

   Comment: _____

3. Describe a time when you voluntarily undertook a special project above and beyond your normal responsibilities.

Expected answer: Did the candidate volunteer for a large task/responsibility despite an already full workload and succeed without undue compromise of other responsibilities? Was there an insignificant, short-term addition, or an unnecessary sacrifice of other areas?

Score: _____

Comment: _____

4. Many people have good ideas, but few act on them. Tell me how you've transformed a good idea into a productive business outcome.

Expected answer: Did the candidate generate a meaningful action plan to bring the idea to reality? Was there a haphazard, unrealistic, or unproductive transformation?

Score: _____

Comment: _____

Index

W

About Adam Haeder

Adam Haeder is one of the nation's foremost experts in Network Administration and Linux technology. A respected instructor and brilliant author, Adam is a Vice President at the prestigious Applied Information Management Institute in Omaha, Nebraska. Expert in Intel hardware and Network Administrator internals, Adam possesses the rare combination of management and technical expertise that is critical to an outstanding IT consultant. Adam is a Linux Certified Administrator (LCA), a Cisco Certified Networking Associate (CCNA), and a Cisco Certified Academic Instructor (CCAI).

About Mike Reed

When he first started drawing, Mike Reed drew just to amuse himself. It wasn't long, though, before he knew he wanted to be an artist.

Today he does illustrations for children's books, magazines, catalogs, and ads.

He also teaches illustration at the College of Visual Art in St. Paul, Minnesota. Mike Reed says, "Making pictures is like acting — you can paint yourself into the action." He often paints on the computer, but he also draws in pen and ink and paints in acrylics. He feels that learning to draw well is the key to being a successful artist.

Mike is regarded as one of the nation's premier illustrators and is the creator of the popular "Flame Warriors" illustrations at **www.flamewarriors.com**. A renowned children's artist, Mike has also provided the illustrations for dozens of children's books.

Mike Reed has always enjoyed reading. As a young child, he liked the Dr. Seuss books. Later, he started reading biographies and war stories. One reason why he feels lucky to be an illustrator is because he can listen to books on tape while he works. Mike is available to provide custom illustrations for all manner of publications at reasonable prices. Mike can be reached at **www.mikereedillustration.com**.